‘Where P

ar

other poems

by

Joseph Goodson

Compiled by
Graham Bell, Stephen Bell and Stephanie Bell
Illustrated by Graham Bell

Published by Graham Bell and Stephen Bell, 2019

Layout: special thanks to Philip Green of Classic Printers

Printed and bound in the UK by Classic Printers (Crowland) Ltd

A catalogue record for this book is available from the British Library.

ISBN 978-1-83853-080-8

Joseph Percival Goodson
(1916 - 2004)

At the War Memorial, Hall Hill, Brigstock
(Photo courtesy of Northamptonshire Telegraph)

When this photo was taken, in 2001, Joseph Goodson, a former soldier, had sounded the Last Post on Remembrance Sunday every year since 1927.

Introduction

Joseph Goodson left his native Nottinghamshire at the age of nineteen to train as a lumberjack at Brigstock Camp, in the heart of Rockingham Forest, bound for Canada. However, he met and married my aunt, Marjorie, and lived in Old Dry Lane, Brigstock, for the rest of his life. He loved his adoptive county of Northamptonshire and its countryside.

A manual worker with a succession of jobs, Uncle Joe had no worldly ambition. But his burly physique belied a sensitive poetic spirit, and he found fulfilment in a creative life: as an amateur musician – principal cornet player in the village band and tenor in the church choir; as an amateur oil painter – focusing on colourful local scenes (some examples of his painting are included to illustrate the poems); but above all he was an exceptional poet – some of his poems have been read on BBC Radio, and in 1971 he was awarded the Certificate of Merit by the International Who's Who in Poetry 'for distinguished contributions to poetry', and he was a founder member of Kettering Poetry Group. He was also an active member of the Workers' Educational Association.

When Nina Steane, a fellow member of the Poetry Group, gave a poetry reading in 1969, describing the English countryside, she chose the work of one poet – Joseph Goodson. By way of introduction to the audience she asked him to give an idea of where he was coming from. Here's an extract:

The Welland Valley with its rose sunsets, its striding viaduct, its smoky horizons seen from Seaton on a summer's evening, may achieve that quintessence a person is permitted – to screw that little extra from living which we call inspiration. These low hills, valley villages and pastoral calms are, I think, an ideal setting for poets and painters or seekers of the spiritual refreshment which comes from solitude.

I believe I had my first hankerings for poetic expression when I was in my teens. We lived at Nottingham then, and I used to love to lie in the long grass at Wollaton Park and gaze through the waving stalks at the fairy towers of Wollaton Hall and dream dreams. It was in 1935 that I came to Brigstock with its lovely church, its stream, its meadow, the green ridings of Fermyn Woods, and the sunsets behind Stanion from the lane where I now live.

Poetry is not always easy to understand, even to those who write it when the frenzy has gone. Yet it is so worthwhile – I wonder, was it the original language man's Maker intended him to use in the beginning?

I once told him that although I didn't always understand his poetry, I loved the sound of it. Timeless in style, to me it has the feel of sentiment and nostalgia, with a touch of humour here and there. It was not unusual for him to rework his poems (see *Bells o' Brigstock* next as an example), making it difficult at times to decide which version he finally intended, but we have tried to make reasoned guesses. Some rationalisation of the lines may have helped the flow too. Where possible the poems have been grouped according to subject, e.g. Brigstock, birds, the countryside, the seasons. All the poems are of manageable length, except three long ones to illustrate something of his versatility; and a witty ditty or two at the other end of the scale.

John Clare, Northamptonshire's 'peasant poet', was Uncle Joe's main inspiration, and the epithet 'a poet is born, not made' could apply to him too. In fact, I sometimes wonder whether the mantle of John Clare fell on Joseph Goodson (cf. *The Thrushes Nest*). When I offered to publish a few of his poems, he declined with characteristic wit: 'No, I'll be famous when I'm dead.' Apart from a booklet of eleven poems (*Wansford Bridge and Other Poems*), published by J. L. Carr in 1968, all of which are included here, and regular entries in the Poetry Group's periodical, too few of them have been in the public domain, so we've assembled this selection as a labour of love to honour his prodigious talent, and I hope you will enjoy reading them over and over again, as I do, and be edified.

'Poeta nascitur, non fit.'

Graham Bell

Bells of Brigstock

~~Who will~~ NOW stand with me awhile,
And hear the bells,—
~~The glorious~~ THOSE VILLAGE bells;
~~Whose lilt and~~ JUST LET THEIR cadence ~~would~~ ALL beguile
As with the breeze
It fades and swells:

The ~~smiling~~ FAR-OFF woods, the ~~singing~~ streams
The pleasing green
THE HAUNTS Where the children played,
~~They all~~ would have ~~less~~ no part it seems
Were Brigstock bells
~~All~~ NOW mute and dead.

The exile in some foreign land
Knows well the paths
~~Of former~~ OF FRIENDS AND sires,
And gazes o'er the burning sand
To dream of home;—
~~Of~~ THESE ringing shires.

~~So trill~~ TURN you bells, ~~trill~~ LIFT sweet and ~~long~~ STRONG,
~~Let your dear music never~~ LET THAT HOME SOUND be done
~~For~~ WHILE all thats good, ~~and sweet~~ THAT'S FOND and true...
~~Fond English hearts still find in you.~~
THAT HEARTS TO HOME MAY FIND WITH YOU

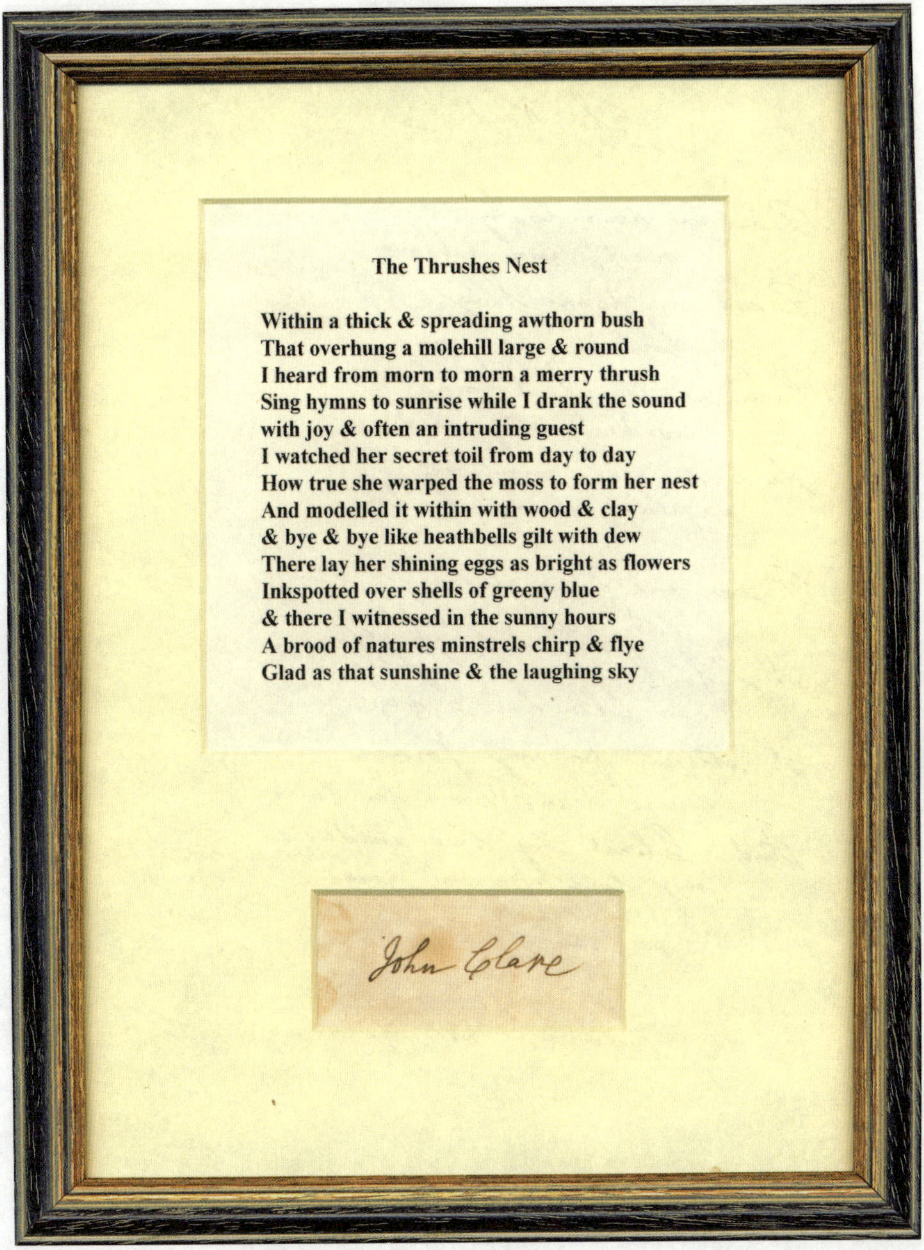

The Thrushes Nest

Within a thick & spreading awthorn bush
That overhung a molehill large & round
I heard from morn to morn a merry thrush
Sing hymns to sunrise while I drank the sound
with joy & often an intruding guest
I watched her secret toil from day to day
How true she warped the moss to form her nest
And modelled it within with wood & clay
& bye & bye like heathbells gilt with dew
There lay her shining eggs as bright as flowers
Inkspotted over shells of greeny blue
& there I witnessed in the sunny hours
A brood of natures minstrels chirp & flye
Glad as that sunshine & the laughing sky

John Clare

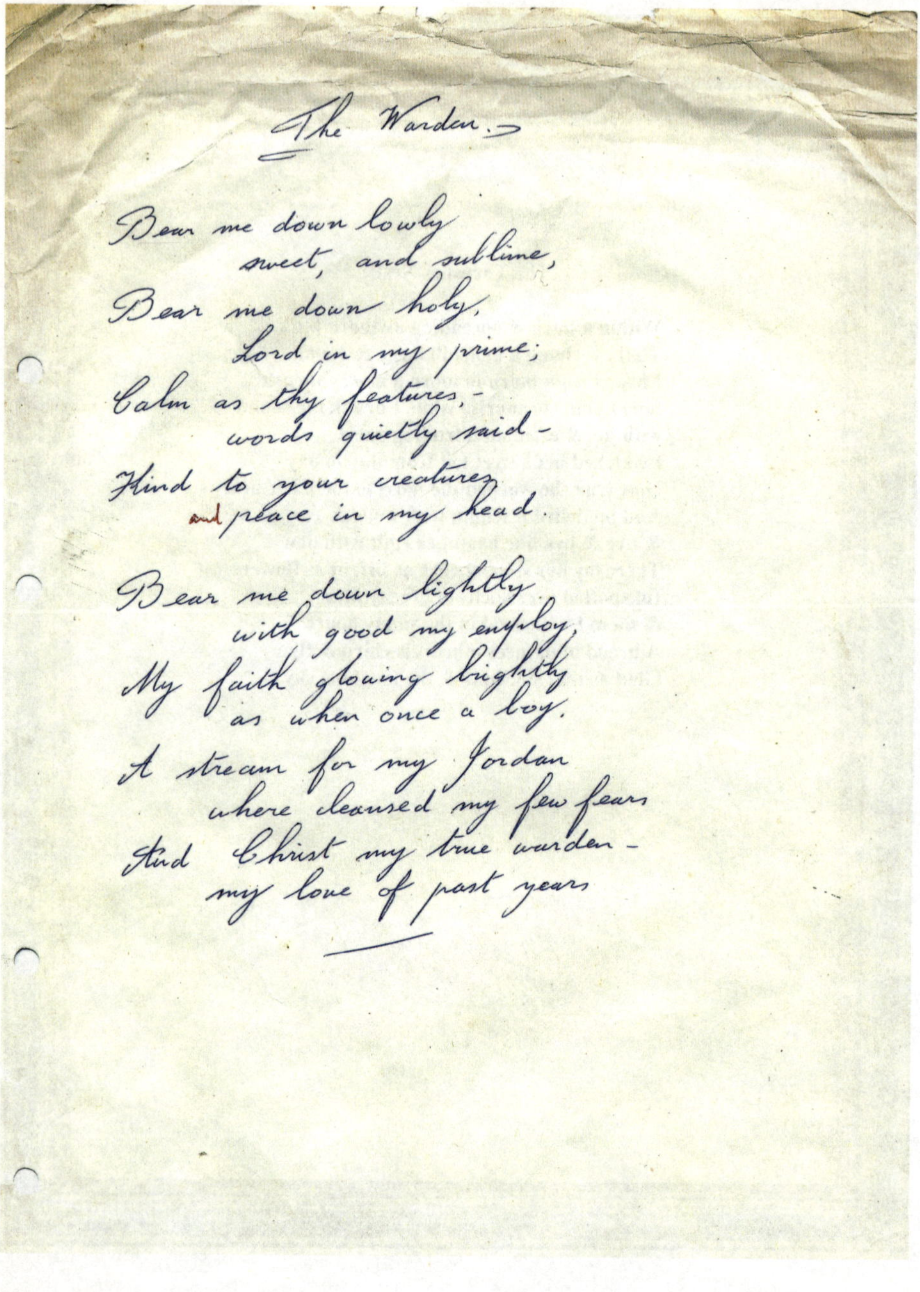

The Warden.

Bear me down lowly
sweet, and sublime,
Bear me down holy,
Lord in my prime;
Calm as thy features,-
words quietly said-
Kind to your creatures
and peace in my head.

Bear me down lightly
with good my employ,
My faith glowing brightly
as when once a boy.
A stream for my Jordan
where cleansed my few fears
And Christ my true warden-
my love of past years

The Warden handwritten

The Poems

Poems marked with * have a note at the end.

Helpston *

Come now the flowers of Eastertide
with ladysmock and cowslip bloom;
and the lily, like some Easter bride
to wait beside the poet's tomb.

Come morning dews like maidens' tears
to fall beside this honey'd stone,
where supreme among his peers
lies Clare – now honoured and alone.

John Clare *

Not for praise of the world
nor words of men,
since these like clouds will pass –
and when the sun
to this one force I knew
extends its beam,
then there the soul of incandescence
beyond mortality,
transcends the dream.

Not for praise of the world
nor laurel'd fame,
since these will wither and pass –
and when my name
in obscure dust
lies with its sire,
it's then perhaps
my solstice lines will burn,
with living flame.

John Clare as a young man

So oft I leave

So oft I leave these crowded ways
to find that favoured spot,
the cottage, cross, the peaceful church,
the limes, the parting pot;
and seeking still I think of thee
who held the crown of fame,
whose work lives on that all may see
the laurels round thy name.

Time can but move and leave its mark
where man has lived his day,
but songs whose roots are the soul
must still define their way;
for who shall pluck those inmost strings
oft scorned by worldly pride,
yet Clare's full joy and sadness brings
what nature's truth implied.

No inspired mind more lucid speaks
than they who sipped that fount,
where genius well'd the fevered thought,
that must o'er all surmount
to leave its aura down the years
and live some after day,
while thro' the vale of want and tears
it sends its burning ray.

Glinton *

Like a needle of silver,
far off across the fenny flats,
we saw the spire – clean, defined;
close to the throbbing highway;
retaining still its oasis charm
in the heat of an age.

It was Easter,
the church beautiful,
the grotesque gravestones warm
and would seem half-minded
to yield their dead
in premature resurrection.
The gold of daffodils –
splashed sunlight –
and in the corner of the church
a tiny sepulchre –
childhood emblem of adult faith.

We leave,
passing the stone mummies
in the porch,
and the village drowses on:
then, in the distance,
the flyer from the north
assaults the level crossing,
and the picture is smudged
with sulking smoke.

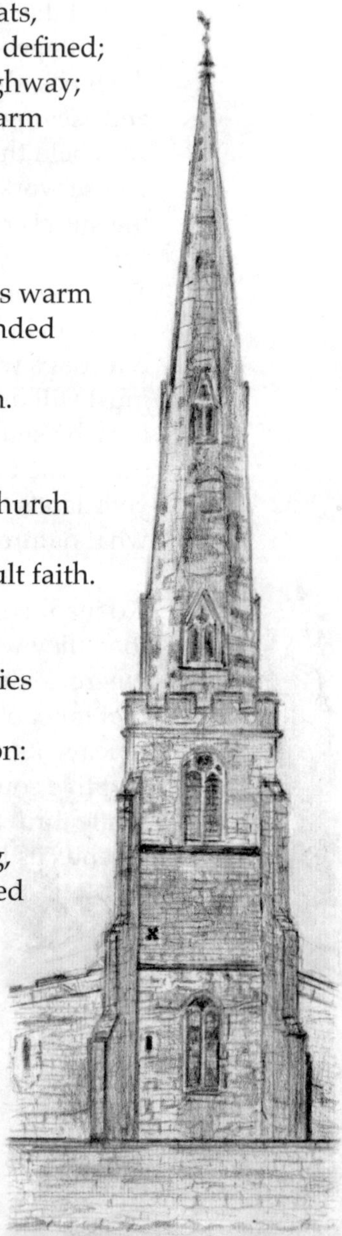

Glinton Church steeple

Fields of England

To have walked the fair green fields of England,
tramped her misted silent woods;
watched her streams of living diamonds,
seen loveliness in her varied moods.

To have heard the birds declare her beauties,
scanned her green and gilded shires;
marched with men to far-off duties,
loved this land of hearts and sires.

Brigstock *

Its very church
is like God's face,
its every tree
a thing of grace;
and every flower
to here imply
that the spirits I've known
can never die.

Its meadow stream
its summer skies,
its wintered woods
its vale and rise,
eternity might claim the soul,
but here such beauty
keeps it whole.

Harper's Brook

By Harper's Brook

For all the springs and golden summers,
the bliss of years and truth;
the bells of home and life's newcomers,
the childhood charms, of youth.

For woods and fields and carefree hours,
and walks by willowed stream;
for eyes which once like early flowers
enticed love's tender dream.

For all the joys, the manhood pleasures,
the heart to its vain pursuit,
life's eldorado bright with treasures,
'til tongues, long loved, are mute.

In gift the eye perceives the glory
where childhood spans to age,
but gentleness takes up the story
across life's mortal stage.

A moment stopped by sacred stone
once touched by the hands of youth,
the memory fades, the world strives on,
but the heart retains its proof.

And so for man, his child and village,
to stand at the roads of change;
the line retrieved from time and pillage,
though hearts and flowers are strange.

Bells o' Brigstock *

Who will stand with me awhile,
and hear the bells,
the glorious bells;
whose lilt and cadence would beguile,
as with the breeze
it fades and swells?

The smiling woods, the singing streams,
the pleasing green
where the children played,
they all could have less part it seems,
were Brigstock bells
all mute and dead.

The exile in some foreign land
knows well the paths
of former sires,
and gazed o'er the burning sand
to dream of home,
of ringing shires.

So trill you bells, trill sweet and long,
let your dear music never be done;
for all that's good, and sweet and true…
fond English hearts still find in you.

A Verse Cameo on Brigstock – its Parish Church of St Andrew and the People Past and Present *

Be still
and heed these stones;
walk gentle, walk slow
where steps lead on
to great distinctions;
these fulgent glories
tempered to ages,
established in stone;
imperishable fact
that faith still lives
though men must go.
What splendours speak
for those who wait,
and to what felicity
the hearts of men,
awhile from rampant scene
in time may see –
all vain conceptions
measured, stilled,
and silence here
more eloquent now
than words of men.

'Long-and-short' stonework
on Brigstock Church

Be still
and heed these stones;
as man was young and hale,
birthed in fault,
so, the misted fen
sent forth its watch,
with book and staff
and the wandering cross
to strike mute earth –
this quarrying birth
for slight demesne,
from lowering glades
rude hands to heave,
to thrust and place
in the measuring sun,
this simple grace.

Be still
and heed these stones;
this market cross,
these cottage homes;
May's child
and garland scene,
each man a boy
by his native stream
and voices heard
while youth was green
in hearts unbruised;
these fronded days,
these ways eternal young
by pool and willow-light.

Market Cross, Brigstock

Be still
and heed these stones;
these bones of time
where spirits have lived,
hearthed in hope,
breathed essence of home.
The mind that stirred
in its native school,
saw visions rare
while hope was young;
and the lads of the green
who sleep like gods,
who wait their call
from foreign fields;
what communal scene
where lives like flowers
had met the sun,
and now have closed
their season done,
all memory blown
like petals from summer gone –
to these late years.

Be still
and heed these stones;
these home-close woods
with message of kings,
of ways once royal –
Plantagenet green;
of the keening horn
and flack of bow,
pennant and panoply –
accoutrements of cross and sword,
of silence green
where Bocase broods
by courts of kings;
could Sherwood's rogue
over Welland's bank
have known the Lowick stream,
this forest monarch bowed at last
in glorious wreck –
where no deer graze?

Bocase Stone

Be still
and heed these stones;
the swinging signs
and gabled walls,
hearths and hearts
and ribald banter,
ambered glass
and bright decanter,
these friendly inns;
this social scene
where loves have crossed
their native green;
of markets, trades,
hopes and fears;
the cavalcade to these late years;
with horse and hound
to make its entry
and peasant liege
in chase with gentry;
the hosts and hearts
and spirits keen
all crossed and left
their native green.

Be still
and heed these stones;
what small dispatch
life's season holds,
men look to home's familiar scene;
a cup of grace,
a toast for loves well known,
a thought which warms
the crowding years;
most excellent hall
where spirits in life
take hope beyond earth's sleep;
calm refuge, treasury green,
enough, for trades and time.

The May Dance *

The stackyard's gone where the children played,
where the youth from the village lay close with the maid;
the cock in the barn and the ducks by the pond,
and the close-by clock with its spire like a wand.

And here is the bridge with the names on stone,
the yesteryear lads to the place they would own;
life's brief encounters moss-hid and unseen;
come a day come a year, their spirits will be green.

And this is the cross where the flowers were arrayed,
where the children of light with their ribbons were displayed;
and the summer'd fields of England were entwined for a day
in an exile's heart, with the children of May.

The Queen of the May

The fields are green, the skies are blue,
and the flowers bloom sweet today,
and England's heart shall never die
while there is a Queen of the May.

Come autumn wind, come winter's flood,
come spring, show summer the way,
this England's heart shall never die
while there is a Queen of the May.

The passing cloud, the singing stream
bring smiles and songs today,
for childhood's heart pays homage too
before the Queen of the May.

Swift growing youth too soon must leave
the green and posied way,
but ageing hearts still come and breathe
their songs with the Queen of the May.

This old grey cross, where through the years
each child hath sung its lay,
the symbol of childhood, of summer's birth…
the throne for the Queen of the May.

O fleeting years could I but hold,
could I but live one day
a child again in the month of flowers,
to homage the Queen of the May.

The Silver Band *

Among rarest talents men may find,
there's few to 'thrall like music's kind.

Let none despise this hutch of sound,
nor each who here by honour bound
aspires through 'Celia's lofty grade
to dignify his humble trade.
The force of splendour shafts a beam
that's fused in a noble dream,
a hope that crystals once the powers
which urge the harvest life endowers.
Vast organs strike the lofty keys
yet fields of glory honoured these,
the men whose eyes beheld the scene
where flowers and children filled the green.
The spark that nerves the heart to fame
seldom flares where few can claim
the laureate splendour learning brings
on fame's uneasy lonely wings.

Man walks once this earthy stage,
he makes his mark upon life's page,
and there he 'quips the simple needs
where friends and music are his deeds;
desiring not the vaster scene
he strains in this, his native green,
the honoured scion of humble mien,
his prize, the rude untutored strain.
No Doric splendour furnished these,
their hall, the field; their pillars, trees;
euphonia's sound and cornet's plaint
here blend the heart in quiet restraint.
Let none despise these lowly chords
for humble start the great awards,
where men hark back to simple things
when power no more its fullness brings.

So empires fall, time changes peers,
but we've kept faith – one hundred years.

Christmas *

Christmas morn –
the humble sound of brass
exalts a Saviour's birth,
spreads the village plain
with lowly praise;
tiers of angels singing
with this man's lowly worth,
and the animals' eyes reflecting
old Bethlehem's gaze.

Old photo of the Band
marching round Brigstock

'Band Concert, Brigstock' by Joseph Goodson

Braybrook's Row *

Only here the eloquence of silence;
this stillness in the sabbath sun –
and nearby, stacked timber and nettles;
the moods of quiet and suspended labour.

Only here the smell of flake-paint,
of window-wood and dust stoop-door entries,
forget-me-nots and border flowers,
the fragrance of a rose like a memory that lingers.

Only shade and shadow; a mind's echoes to prophecy;
words for incantation from window-wise faiths;
only this time and a turn to remembrance;
a year to its thoughts like a page turned –
a conclusion of regrets.

'Braybrook's Row, Brigstock' by Joseph Goodson
(No.1 is the first house beyond the fence.)

Derelict Cottages (Braybrook's Row, Brigstock) *

By these stairs, to have stood in a stone shell;
the soul and the spirit gone, the place condemned:
alone, and yet to have lived,
to have known a heart's employ
in matters of living, of love, and of things cherished
in the structure of a nation, village, and the homage of hearts;
these things may not perish where men remember
and keep to their weal the way of friends –
the fond mysteries and images of home.

By these stairs, to have smelt the odours
of a summer's riot; the flowering of herb
and garden bloom; and from the small casements
to have heard the cuckoo's note;
that morning note aswell with sound
on a May's cool breeze;
and here to have heard the soothe of bees
as they drift with their loaded wealth;
and to have known the health of mind men feel
when light their cares –
when brief their stairs.

Up these stairs, to a hallowing
the chime of steepled tower;
and by chaptered stone
the hearts of the village to lie;
the clock to its beat for a measure of four
and a misted dawn; the stream's wraith –
hid, the cattle quiet, and the world in first wonder
to a flecking of dew, on thorn.

By these stairs, not dead the prayers of the children,
nor of hearts; all are to their parts
in life's odyssey of souls:
but not here the loss nor the dereliction,
though a cottage may fall; but by a stair and a wall
to stand with the craftsmen and the ghosts;
for just awhile to wait and to watch
with the Creator, the Presence, and all.

By these stairs, in honour to have stood;
to have felt the strength, the grace, and the fealty
of a nation in a statesman's voice;
to have seen Coventry haloed and brave
to its night of fire; and to have sensed
the huge forces in honour bound,
resolute and quiet to remembering
with the humble and the great.

Up these stairs, to have heard Christmas rampant
to frosted light; the cries of children
with their delight at the wealth of gifts;
white drifts of snow ledge-high;
pristine and levell'd for racing feet,
for the fun of the young complete
and heedless of time:
while across the limitless and dazzling plains of snow
the cowman stumbles and calls to his frolicking herd.

By these stairs, to have heard in a night's suspense the awaited cry,
the hour when birth had at last eased all;
the midwife's call, and the croon of the mother to her wrinkled joy;
a girl, a boy, who cares! The night is done and there's peace in the house;
the man is to his dreams, his tea, and his crackling grate;
and things are quiet, to the rise of the sun.

Up these stairs, stirs the vision of yesterday's child;
the marks on the wall, the scribble,
the nails where the photographs hung;
the faded paint, the curtain hook, and beneath –
the door to the potato store:
and now, no more the spark nor the say of a name;
no child, no call nor game nor warmth of home;
no move where the light now falls
and slants to shadow and shade.

Up these stairs, so many echoes, so many voices,
so many feet to have come: the relative, the doctor,
the priest, the friend; and the stones impregnate
with the prayers of spirits past;
a cast of actors unknown nor sought of a wider stage,
but the script legible and illuminate with life,
for they who would see.

Up these stairs, at the day's end,
the man to his wife; to comfort of arms,
quiet talk and the brief interlude before sleep;
love's haven where the cares of union are resolved;
or left to beyond the reef of night, the lagoon of rest;
to the coming of tomorrow with its sun, its hope,
its strengthening of bonds.

By these stairs, as a year turned late,
to have been where the women came hushed;
the two from the village who would lay out the dead;
and the house made quiet of that fell dread
where the children are still; awed by loss
and the pent shock where the will is for tears;
and hearts are to wreckage in the blighted time
of a love's long fears.

By these stairs, to have stood in the cold blear time
of a fading night;
a star in the east set on the brow of day,
to its lifting light;
and here to have heard the creak and the click of wood,
of folk in sleep; the murmur of a child to its dreams,
the breathings and slight move
of things well loved.

The Boxing Day Hunt *

The varied east has dawned its dying wind,
and the Christmas hour has sipped the Christ-owned wine,
but wine shall fang with blood this sleeping morn
when flecking death surmounts pale pity's line.

A valley's mist has birthed the baying hound,
swift harbinger of crowd, of plunging horse,
round tally, round tally the straight horn flares its sound
and the strong blood strains through a times old veined course.

Far from horizoned woods runs the raving fox
on by the silent streams of a crisping morn;
dry leaves stir in a hedgerow's stale retreat
and crimson flecks with scarlet in the thorn.

'The Meet, Brigstock' by Joseph Goodson

The Old Dry Lane *

I love this lane!
The old stone lane
that seems to lead to nowhere;
I love each bush,
each nest and tree,
and the village down below there.

And many's the morn
I'd meet the dawn
up there alone with fancy;
and waiting hear,
when the hour is clear,
birds call at light's infancy.

I'd hear the peewit,
watch the stoat
make sport beneath the brambles;
and o'er the hedge
see rabbits play
twelve feet from where death gambols.

I've seen the hunt
with horses shorn
ride by on Boxing Morning;
and in the evening
heard the horn
peal out its stirring warning.

And then in June
I'd see the rose
surmount each hedge in glory;
no sweeter thing
did God compose
than that enraptured glory.

When far from home
one way I'd mind,
one way through life's sojourning
that leads me still
this lane to find,
this lane to home returning.

'Old Dry Lane, Brigstock' by Joseph Goodson

The High Way *

Quiet ways from life's mad rush,
time to think midst nature's blush;
still'd these thoughts, more still the heart,
where Christ and the living waters start.

Hours pass, no sound to breach
the soul's repose or nature's speech;
a citadel found 'long earthy path,
with Christ to find the cooling draught.

Fairest morn with eyes to see
the glory of God in many a tree;
for a lifelong hope a tear could shed,
but Christ he calls to the greening mead.

Years come and eyes grow dim,
yet light have I enough in him;
this aching frame condemned to fall,
in Christ my soul to find its all.

Track from Old Dry Lane
towards Straight Riding

Straight Riding *

Frost-laced woodsides and light slow breaking;
chilled territories fixed in retreats of silence:
only the spoors where quiet marauders
had paced through shadow;
left the trails of the night beneath a late white moon.

Pillars of pine dark thrilled in silence;
cathedral calm to flake-drift, and fall;
and here, from winter's pall the squirrel,
the bared empyrean, scuts, sparks a bough
to lace with light this cold east window of the world.

Far-off are sky sounds, stringing and wild,
where wayfarers in the sun ride the geese roads
clanging their chilled calls;
and deer on the ridings frost-antlered to freedom,
statued in stillness, down keen glaced aisles.

'Straight Riding' by Joseph Goodson

Straight Riding *

Time for the lonely lark, and the gloam of the nightingale,
time for sunrise – the lifting prayer of the fields,
time to stop amidst the day's turbulence,
and to assess the spirit against the profit of the world;
time for sunset and for meditation, the calm that measures the man,
time to value one's place in the meaning of the universe,
time to be still before the humbling forces of creation,
time for beauty and for knowledge, the eternity of truth,
time to be gentle – until there is no more of time.

On Silver Hill *

Praise God for his angels in hedgerow and tree,
for the yellowhammer, the blackbird, the bullfinch, the bee;
praise him for the promises seen of his hand,
that for man all paradise is loose in the land.

Praise for the thicket, for holly and thorn,
field poppies like flame in the blush of the dawn;
stand praise at the forest – in sun-sceptred light
with gold-gilded leafways still wet from the night.

Praise life for its hours where men, though alone,
may rise in earth's stature to heaven and a throne;
to have snatched the fine moment where the heart in all things
ascends like a bird on light-lifted wings.

Make praise amidst loss, amidst ruin and time,
'til the last pale kingdoms are to rubble and lime;
make praise in the heart 'til the heart no more
may sing and exalt what it's known well before.

Sawmill *

Sheer cut, severed, sweet flesh of trees;
piled hulk-harvest, beast-dragged, broke.
Limb-lopped, fallen, the pillars of kings;
pole-nudged, bodged to whirled shark steel:
such winds that winnow the hedgerow traps –
they whistle by girth and board gaps.

Rucked bark, elephantine crimped;
bulk silent, meek as mice;
stripped sheered flesh, white as milk;
fleered, straight ripped to uniform shape:
Tyburn massed, tall nettles stand,
and violets edge the sawdust strand.

Swung flung hook, priest-bowed steel,
burdens borne down shackling chain;
where huge death lies men hop like fleas,
steer earth's gods with practised hand –
an acorn dropped in a far-off year
is a solemn thought, by a forest peer.

The Small Friends *

Ranee, Badger, Judy
and Tony, Charlie and Ben – the dogs;
Fluff, Bidby, Benny, Bessie
and two Pennys – the cats.
Only animals,
and faithfulness, happiness, trust,
friendship, loyalty, the delight of their living;
and the apprehension of their so limited time,
the pain of their passing.

'The Friends' by Joseph Goodson

Golden Labrador *

Never a word –
but eyes like pools of love's compassion;
language at times to make absurd
man's trivial talk;
to skip the fashion of doubtful friends,
whose happy bond soon amends
all human frailties –
Just Judy! The gold of Heaven
for a few short years on loan to man.

Judy

The Organ Blower *

What joys are mine that here I blow,
and the organ breathes the tunes that I know;
where Madonna lilies they enscent the air,
while the birdsong at even it holds not one care.

'Tis the evening hymn the heart would soothe,
and as from the world would my spirit enmove;
and here steadied reason with such thought sublime
portrays this life's theme to the ending of time.

In whose dusted solitude would I ply the shaft,
worn smooth by other hands who long now have passed;
in manhood's full strength it is humble I feel
at those spirits now gone who in here did kneel.

I've tasted excitement, the thrill of the chase,
but here I found peace and God's welcome grace;
I saw the clouds open, thro' the window came light,
and here in my solitude I knew God was right.

Weathercock *

Set, gilt and bright, up there,
to the peripheries of light;
the lone sentinel to range over field,
farm, and things made strange
in the affairs of men;
what cares now or then
to have proved all chance and change
in time and weathers;
what hopes, what aspirations to lie
like feathers by broods of men
grown old and gone.
So, life is to its seasons:
to first-bud and flowering, seed-fall, and frost;
and still for man his fret of mind, his schemes,
his way through the hours – his lot.
A named stone his proof and demise;
and yet, of these to rise redeemed
and whole beyond the crowings of betrayal
whilst time shall endure
before the cross on a hill.
How cold now your gleam
to this lowering sun; and a following star
to be your watch through the shrouds of night;
but what of tomorrow –
some thread of light to have herald the dawn;
and then again reborn the ways of village,
of town and shire?
Then myths and motives to perpetuity
through a compass of days,
and you proud Chanticleer aloft as ever
in the brightening of the rays.

Down a Country Road *

This is the way of the silent round
with a backing wind to frozen ground;
of thickets cleared and lately breached
the broken fence, now tight and pleached.

Here are ways through frost and snow
where red fox moves and few men go;
where the far-off note of a belling hound
drifts, then fades with haunting sound.

These are the woods where streams are mute,
where the misted stag takes a silent route;
the way where winter, shouldering all,
broods dark and still to the red sun's fall.

This is the bridge where the lads I have known
had made their mark on ivy'd stone;
a late-year relic with time so brief
to have left but this, small pride's relief.

Here are the plots where simple hands
had nurtured seed for small demands;
life's slight relief from hearth and home
with labouring sweat to native loam.

For each a place where hope or fears
distils the best in life and years,
the tender thought, the scenes of joy
still loved and known as when a boy.

Come all the schemes, the lust for powers,
these yet are less than wayside flowers;
when plan and structures change and fall –
the weed alone adorns the wall.

What more to need than this the day
where spans the sun to its fading ray,
to have felt the force which proves the need
that man with God, is kin indeed.

The Team

The lads of the village have played away;
they went to the war that some might say
they were heroes, and to be honoured
in a future day.

They went, game-heart, with the teams of death
and no more in the green their frosted breath;
no more at home their prowess to display –
the colours of the village have played away.

Home's wayside flowers still come, arrayed;
though cold the kiss of mother and maid:
so brief the years at the village school,
so brief their time to craft and tool.

The names now left on post and stile
have aged beyond their youth and guile;
yet those same names fond memory keeps
'til the laurel unwinds, and the trumpet sleeps.

Slight the accounts with line and pen
to have judged the prides and faults of men;
yet false the judgements war has made
where hearts in tidied fields lie laid.

Slow turns a year with the wheel of time,
and life to forfeit – though hope, at prime;
a time for schemes, a plan for affairs,
'til men, with war, concede their cares.

New Dawn

Turn not long from the light;
the reaching shadows that lie before
are yesterday's dreams, and waking schemes,
known once as the hour was bright
lie with that day whose brief appointments
count no more.

Turn not long from the light;
life's common field is warm with friends
and only hearts and hope
can solve these gnarling threads,
for all have broken ends –
knotted fragments
from that splendid hue
whose cloak had garbed past days.

Turn not long from the light,
for what the night may bring
time yet will move
and set for man his fretful dawn,
while trades of earth will lie like dust
by the hearth of age
and portalled fame grow cold
in the minds of the young.

The Everlasting Wonder

There was a time
when I had watched with wonder
the flights of the dawn;
where I had seen those vistas
I'd thought not to inherit
of this earth-course birth,
but there beyond reasoning
to have walked
as of a truth's inheritance
by bluebell drifts
and to have drawn the breath of the gods
to joy's excess in those scented glades.

There was a time
when the eyes were clear
for light and loveliness,
where pleasures are told but once
by men amidst the treasures of youth;
where the hair of a girl was divine
and to sweet madness and whisperings,
and quickened hearts
were to hauntings of paradise
with words and kisses to promises for life,
and the clasp which grows faint
only to the bruisings of time.

There was time
for that dulcet note
of the spring-borne hope
for which men wait in their autumn years,
where tears are not for loss but renewal
in gift where memory holds the latch
of the mind supernal
in praise before the brightening rays.

There is time
where held the charisma
of living to the brow
clutching the star of understanding,
and where the dead are not lost
of earth's vain time
by the light of the spirit's flame;
but there at the trove of utterance
to a prayer from the frescoes of night,
before the dawn and the first bud flowers
and to no doubt at the requiem of loss
for beauty and innocence,
but on and ever to the lasting wonder.

And then the world shall be young

And then the world shall be young
and there will be no more death;
no more shall the furrow slight the brow
nor the curl have shade of sober years;
the eyes will keep their summers
and the foot shall not stray from the stream,
nor leave the Lord-blest shade
of the child's own singing green.

Sweet will come the night
with Christ and his holy stars,
and the former fragments will rise
like fire from the Canaan field;
and graves shall give their ghosts
at last made holy,
and the woman sleep calm with child
in the blessing of the genesis flesh.

Who Would Stand

O who would stand with me
and hear the thousand throated choirs,
the drone of bees, the lilt of birds,
the meadow's whispering spires,
the chiming bells on a sabbath morn,
and the brooding ringdove's call?
All these in moments bring to me
some joy surpassing all.

The murmuring stream that burbles by
'neath many a crumbling span,
and gathering yet more music sweet
than where its spring began;
until no more its rushing theme
is heard by you, or me…
but all that lusty foam at last
has found the waiting sea.

Before the Sun *

Who has seen the sky in glory,
the subtle shades of moon and cloud,
the world endowed when gone the day
with this vast stage, this vaulted scene,
where stars await the riding night,
the wheeling light that shafts to the eye of man;
the timeless void where began this act of truth,
this endless proof of system, order, scheme;
the dream, the privilege once perhaps of mortal minds
when blinds of death let loose their lowering shades;
and glades unseen, nor lit by earthling suns,
at last are known.
This night, this sable curtain poised to the final act;
this ever refuge loaned of the day-spun star.

A Way of Reckoning

And God gave man to sweat by his brow,
to weary himself amidst vagaries of weathers
and the tillage of soil;
by the same token, and because he was merciful,
he gave him great silence for reflection and thought;
he gave him the communion of sun and air,
the fruit of orchard and field,
the strength which surpasses all grief
and which brings him often to the altar of light,
to the intimacy of words which are more than ordinary.
By the stoop of labour,
he has shown man a way of contentment,
the power of reason where simplicity defies the cleverness
of the manipulators – the over-smart.
Amidst the schoolings, the temporal honours of the world,
he gave the illiterate peasant the power and beauty of poetry,
the dignity of family loyalty, the ear for the reflections of age.
In this small allotment of days man need not fear for his time;
a glance at the stars by night,
the love and devotion in human eyes,
the compassion and understanding of mature friends,
the innocence of infants, composed age among flowers,
the steady eyes of a full man seated from labour.
These are not transitory nor a chance of time;
these are the conditions which precinct eternity.

Quarries *

Earth.
Green gouged;
marzipan seam of packed blue boulder,
stone studded in the throes
of a time's old movement.
Crumbled clay, cragged oolite;
land let loose in orchestration vast,
volleying blast, pneumatic drill
and opencast desolation.
Whining phantasies tuned,
swaying to the wired jib,
the lattice-work boom
in the long-lost wood
where the toothed bucket grabs
for a forest's feet.
Rough red rock, sampled, weighed,
dispatched to the iron-skirt maidens,
the high horned breasts,
the hot madonnas
of scrambling economy.

Blast furnace

Serration of furrow, scattered slabbed rock;
feather of larch, of withering pine,
precarious holding each lunar line.
Pickled dead sleeper, cast iron chair,
relics of old companies,
lost in the amalgamations of year '22,
of industrial castration, of nationalisation.
Bright vein of metal on flat ferrous floor;
signal plume of bright Welsh wealth,
there the saddle tank haulier heaves high tubs
from the final raper in the gaping womb.
Ruck and high change, strange harvest and scene;
nature in carnival where powerlings have passed.
As the minotaur tread obliterates the green
man argues with profit, and the garden is dead.

Joseph's sketch of a saddle tank locomotive

Welland Valley *

In the Welland vale time turns slow,
and where the systems of men move easy
among spires and towers,
and when the sun lies low on Seaton hill
only the sounds of cattle disturb still acres;
and the very air is steeped with gentleness
where men long measured and soil –
and corn and beast had closed broad hands in grace
and in churchyards lie.

In the Welland vale a mind can heal,
and thoughts which the hectic town denies here,
may flow in train; and solitude breathes the prayer
no mind could phrase except it feels that force
which quickens – when men are still.

In the Welland vale where the horizons mist,
brown stone stands warm and lanes wind calm
with spirits of men; and even there
the vaulting lines of girdered power,
the viaduct chain stands mellowed with weathers –
the play of time.

Harringworth viaduct

Wansford Bridge *

Here I stand on the still small bridge,
lulled in the silence and the wild bee's humour,
noting the stones, the old stout pointing,
the rusting plate, an old scab which says
'Traction Engines must not cross this Bridge'.

Beneath are the prints where enterprise walked,
the old shallow cutting where navvies slaved
for pride, and beer.
The sleepers are roused now from old-world slumbers,
and the slim vein gone from the impermanent way.

There is no soot on the lip of the arch,
no coupling clank nor squeal of flange;
only foxglove, ragwort, bosoms of May blossom
and the little grey station – the pitiful excuse –
with washing hanging out,
and the old bowed man with his 'Great Northern' cap,
his main line memories.

Fotheringhay *

The kestrel poised in the mild wind's courses
scans the scene of ancient forces,
knows no sound of the whispering green
nor the crimson seal of the murdered queen.

Strange as the errors in each communion
death secures for man his union,
councillors, concepts, gilt and sheen
leave the mounded hope of a wandering queen.

The price of realm for a red king's daughter
leads in faith to fire and slaughter,
and the way of power accepts no loss
when the sword is raised – and seen as a cross.

Meadows, lanes, and easy streams
defy high faith's pastoral schemes,
yet, can the Church define its way –
or Jordan run by Fotheringhay?

France and Scotland vague as history
shade the lanes of England's mystery,
the blood-stained Church with huge refrain
awaits the billowing sheets of Spain.

Standards marked with mural'd story
droop like flowers in fields of glory;
death accepts one queen's request
and Peterboro' shrines the Catholic's breast.

The fires of zeal must yet grow cold,
since varied paths find but one fold;
yet priests and prelates robed for glory –
in royal crimson scribe their story.

Collegiate remnant, mystic mood,
vast pomp that leaves death's ghostly rood;
shall Fotheringhay in covenant stand
'til Herod, or Christ, take Mary's hand.

Castle mound

That Loving Chapter *

That loving chapter's closed,
the nation mourns;
a life, full long composed
beneath its thorns.

Monarchs have held the torch
to glory's flame;
but none shall dim the cross
beside thy name.

Truly didst thou follow
the King of kings,
who takes thy hand at last
by healing springs.

King George VI

At the Passing of a Beloved Monarch *

Our Sovereign Lord King George the Sixth
of Blessed Memory

The everlasting wisdom has ordained
that this rare soul, his earthly service done,
shall leave the peoples over whom he reigned
for other service at a higher throne,
where life's rewarders sing at triumph won
in nobleness attempted and attained
through years more terrible than any known.

What is a nation's love? No little thing:
a vast dumb tenderness beyond all price;
surely a power of prayer upon a wing;
the living anguish of a hope to heal
offered by all hearts here in sacrifice
to spirits bowed in sorrow for the King
that it may touch, to comfort or anneal.

May this devotion help them in their grief;
may the devotion kindle to resolve
to make this stricken country green with leaf,
glad with another hope to be again
a sun about which singing orbs revolve,
a kingdom grown so worthy of her Chief
that millions yet unborn shall bless her reign.

Airfield (Grafton Underwood) *

Only silence, distance,
and a world of solitude
to thread a thought,
with the wheatear and the chaffinch
by this hewn stone;
a quiet commission,
simple as a wayside flower
amidst the truth
and the logic of the old –
the lost conclusions.

Here, among sheep and a poised kestrel
over a stumble of barns,
laughter leaves echoes
from the drawling years;
this drab licence
of dimmed homesteads;
a farm rolled back
from the carpets of concrete
where hawks of retribution assembled,
pawn-leased down the runways of thunder.

By corps had they come,
well-trucked and tidy;
of no alien race
with their hoist and their tackle;
a pocket full of dollars
and turn with the girls
and the nights to grow quiet
from those brief encounters,
till mornings broke loud
with the B-17's.

This rock, commemorative,
rough-stoned in silence;
the postscript left
from the laughter of the young;
and the green fields of Grafton
harrowed from memories
with only the old
to remember the song;
and those bannerheads of youth
in the mutilated skies.

'B-17 over Grafton Airfield' by Douglas Bell (nephew)

Grafton Underwood (Airfield) *

They came to England;
and from her mild dawns
flew to the raging skies of wasted lands.
Not theirs the close acclaim of home or ties,
but for them only this,
that men born free still see what truth implies by faith –
by blood and bond of ancient line.
Remember them;
remember the names they leave behind
along with our own in England's green;
mute testimony of their vital and generous stay;
the way of youth unto manhood marked in stone;
and quietened hearts here to make pause –
in the pass of years.
No tears need they who had frontiered the heavens,
who had ranged from prairied land, mountain, and great rivers
for freedom's sake;
who had risen with the morning flights as eagles
to redeem bright truth;
and in youth to have raised banners like the statements of God –
from earth's dark shades.

Memorial Stone
at Grafton Airfield

Memorial window
in Grafton Church
(photo: Jim Worthington)

Rothwell Crypt *

A devil's bakehouse this with bones to rank,
white skulls like loaves in batch,
devoid of leaven of life;
and more, in death's dungeon
to wait the kindling flame –
the spark which once had fired with hope
their risen clay.

What chilled assemblies these,
where bones of men in calm agreement
lie close-piled to scheme;
all faults unsolved to wait
midst damp and fust;
and factions stable
with death's mute herd
to subscribe no thought,
no probing of mind;
from flesh once quick,
some learned, some great,
but here, stacked and still.

What lost opinions these
to charnel shades,
what class distinctions
heaped to count no more;
proud sire with serf,
arms with other men's wives
and none disturbed,
since all must grin and bear –
where the spider wisps its webs
where things now past unite.

Lincoln Cathedral

Among majesty in stone;
to what presence these earth-small wanderings;
ethereal splendours, spandrel'd glories;
huge statements made through mists of time
for all our ponderings;
this glory, ephemeral beauties lit,
bright-shot with light;
rare manifestations risen in clear cut stone;
what temporal footings here might discharge
the loftier thought;
men have made in substance the sheer long praise
sparked in glass their earthbound wonder.

What majesty in stone enthrals the mind;
that moment's reason hailed where things stand great;
dispels the way of condemnation:
man stands small by his making hand,
yet the awesome presence of faith-long wonder
ensures his way; reveals the clue in earth-poor stone
his road, and his eternity.

The Wonder

No kings, no princes,
no prelates there;
no entourage of pomp
nor graces most fair:
only Joseph with Mary –
and the child to their care,
and the oxen wide-eyed
to that birth most rare.

No exultation, no clamour
nor fuss of fame;
no worldly distinction
to that one blessed name:
just a star to appointment
and God come to earth;
and the heavens to all wonder
with Christ, and his birth.

The Witness *

Were those the hands most practised and sure
in that night of the bright star; and of that crude stall
to have been for the cleanse and swaddle
of such primacy of birth?

Was she, of her worth invest of such care,
such preparation there to have knelt in adoration
before opinions of patriarch, prince,
or the exalted gifts of kings?

Was it for her, the woman,
there to have been with the maid most holy,
predestined among women for that first handling
of man's redemption; of life, hope, and regeneration
beyond the driven nails, the cross,
and the known judgements of Easter?

Was she, exalted of her humility there
to be beyond favours of shepherd, drover or camelmen;
and to have warmed in that mercy of a faith's fine moment,
having beheld those beginnings
such as give credence to love, purpose,
and the divine simplicity of that infant holy truth?

Was she, with the man Joseph, the beasts,
and the blessed woman of the child to be for this one act;
this attribute of supreme gentleness
which could defy the Herodic fears
of calumny and circumstance,
knowing the legions, host-girthed, at their armouries
to lay siege on the cradles of innocence?

Was it for her in that low stall
to have been witness before the world, in such humility;
such service as would defame the pomp, the drape,
and the complexities and confusion of all later edicts?

Will she be remembered of the assessments
when the stall was razed, and for nothing,
in the conflagration where the temples of usury and falsehood
were to lie scattered?

Will she, once there, again be of that silence when time is done;
and will it be for her alone to take the hand of him, once child,
and to reveal before the Judge at the last tribunal
what men had reviled?

Straw

The world and its birthday
lies waiting in straw;
and men, again to their tales
and their telling once more,
speak leagues beyond time;
and child day lifts
the orb of innocence,
sees the head-star bright
on the braid of night,
where moments rare to calm
await the infant wail
that beast and motherhood
wraithed in straw –
might gaze on God.

All earth seems still,
and the birds in the thorn
sit quiet and hushed,
waiting, waiting;
and soon the waking bells
lift high their throats –
clang this praising morn
by hill and field,
where beast and lowliest form
stand dumb in wonder;
and then, the light –
the head-star fading;
day come bright
to the infant story,
the way of the lowly,
the way of the glory;
the beast, the kings,
the man, the maid;
and God – and straw.

When man
by proof
of grace
forsakes
his schemes, redeems
this patent hope one
star alone foretold;
and lone, amidst his
peers rejects life's
fleeting
fame; and
would by
truth in-
vest his
Saviour's
name; all
things a
while in
vanity' s
whims he
sees, yet
knows by
strength
within, a
calm and
ease

Easter

Wait the magic moment,
since like a butterfly
new leased in spring weather –
it will pass by.

Wait, where yellow diadems
drift the wood green,
as light-forms of innocence
which the child had seen.

Wait the blessed moment
aware at full praise,
that the flower-hosts of Easter
hold the Saviour's gaze.

Wait the magic moment,
since like a butterfly
new leased in spring weather –
it will pass by.

One Good Friday

With the coming of this day's light
are we aware of the portent of past events;
only then are the dictates and anomalies
of our common humanity apparent
before the dearth of our spiritual conceptions;
and of the mood of one brooding hour
here to stand contrite –
heavy with the force of our failure
in the blight of past or present judgements.
Only with a cool wind
that wafts a scarecrow on the hill at first light
do we concede to a whisper
that the message of the One-in-Three
was not to be the demise in that one death
of all spirit, hope, conception, fault,
of wonder of mind and process of regeneration.

Only a child that blancoes its Easter shoes
to white in the morning sun;
and an old man who hobbles to church
and sits solitary as he has done through his years –
only these have no peers in time past or time present
to shun by the silence they seek
in forbearance of submission before the consciousness of folly;
only for them in the quiet of centuried structures
are hints and deliberations of prophecy
to speak beyond the common eloquence of men;
and there amidst the imagery and beatitudes
of their simple teachings is credence eternal and sure
above the confederacies, the contention,
and the confusion of their times.

Only after the calamity and contradictions of known history,
or the corruption and mortification of change
do men perceive and delineate the brief context of their humanity;
and only in the honesty of humility are they aware
that hope and fulfilment in earth's time was not to be enough,
and that a child should not be condemned of its father's fault,
nor the judge licensed except he be subject to the tribunals
of persuasion and doubt: the way of Calvary was only for once
amidst the ferment, anguish, and deliberations of men;
and the garden of the first paradise was not to be lost to wilderness
where the wayward years, by the shadows on the hill,
were as a prelude to the flowering of all these Eastertides.

Easter Day 1969 *

Man's history
is a puff of desert wind,
his battalions
slight movements of the grains;
and still there is a seeing,
the awareness beyond flesh
of liege with the beginning:
this Christ-beckon hour
of the permissive brief
with the world gone away
down the vale of its Sabbaths,
and Siloah's head-springs
sweet once more
to the last miracles.

Issues and Lovers

This life's waste
is the whim of lovers;
yet, in the new green bud
I have watched
for my own resurrection;
I am one with the deep mystery
of the mastering of the universe
and yet suspect in this mortality
my birth, my purpose, my end.

Vain the man who says
there is no God;
who arbitrates his mind
with timeless things;
the flesh will clothe the fool
and the angel form,
but this life's waste
is the whim,
the chance of lovers.

Follow Me *

Seeing the two men, the fishers;
of lonely deliberation
he knew his need,
and of the two words,
with no other sound
but knock of boat and tackle,
they let fall their nets,
and heedless of all –
they followed him.

The Minds of Men

The minds of men are hard to trace,
so headlong is their eager race
for pomp and power;
they miss all beauty's mirror'd face
in spring's young flower.

The greatest wealth that man can know
is with him wheresoe'er he go,
if he but sees –
and speaks with God while here below
on bended knees.

Sally Army *

All those captains, all those soldiers;
not a bullet or a gun, nor a sword between them;
for where are they with the world at their shoulders
and a flag and a book, and one Lord they know?

Probe the long shadows, seek out the broken,
onward, ever onward, watch how they go:
firm and unchanged, beyond bargain or token,
pass the quiet legions with the one Lord they know.

(Logo used by permission of TSA)

Music

Drink, my heart, at these pure springs,
assuage life's stress where music brings
some full atonement clear to earth –
to praise with sound a soul's rebirth.

Drink deep the draught of tramps or kings
or silent list' for nature's wings,
where tremulous sound spills down from throats
to fill the fields with heavenly notes.

Be still, my heart, be still, yet seek
this language diverse races speak,
this linking tongue that yet shall raise
in mouths of men – a Saviour's praise.

To Handel

Handel hath struck in me the chord
that brings a man before his Lord,
and lifts above that span of time
where heavenly thought would dwell sublime;
whose noble mood, ecstatic theme,
soars up above each earthward scene;
and heeding not eternal night
lifts high the torch of inward sight,
where orchestration's full refrain
he heard and wrote in mighty strain;
and would earth's circumstance command
with music from some promised land –
O mighty Handel honoured thee,
who saw in blind humility.

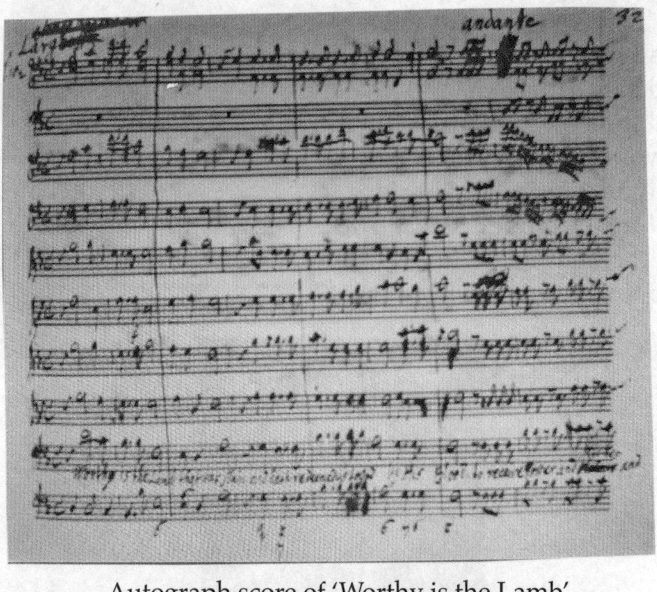

Autograph score of 'Worthy is the Lamb',
the final chorus of *Messiah* (1742)

For Kathleen Ferrier *

Only brief is the utterance of Heaven,
only rare the utterly divine;
speech, song and words,
these are the keys permitted to man;
vision of the immortals
ranged in fleeting splendour
to earth's small pilgrimage;
glorious cavalcade –
a moment's heed amidst the noise,
the poise of beauty manifest, great beyond words,
stirring the ordinary to conscious longing
through mist and eddies of time.

Heaven and larks are sure in creation,
and only man in the fretful days must stand in awe;
dumb, awhile, from clack of trades seeking aids,
truth holds beyond price;
this happy virtue chanced like childhood thoughts
when minds are clean.

Grace is timeless,
and ears grown deaf to loveliness soon respond,
and the voice now tuned with Heaven's choirs
leaves echoes in the fading chords.
Only the living grow cold
and turn from felicity of truth;
the theme is ageless – for ever young,
and loveliness will not dim.

Dylan Thomas *

Yours was the immortality,
the gatherings
of the priest-high hills,
where bosoms of estuary
and the seabirds flute
sound lone their long requiem.

No word of mine
may match their grief,
yet tears were mine
in the spumed panoramas
of your being's intensity,
of the youth who has scorned
fleshed age,
whose kestrel note hangs poised
in a morn's cool wind.

Francis Thompson *

Such are to waste and die
in earth's poverty,
who had looked just awhile
on the riches of Heaven.

Thoughts on St Francis of Assisi *

I believe his simplicity, humility, and greatness of faith
to be the key to that splendour of mind which now lives on,
long after its earthly husk has fallen from the soaring spirit.
In him there was none of seeking for vain expression,
nor that vulgarity one finds in men, who, in pride,
would deify themselves by their ceaseless scratchings
in this earth's common dust.
He had seen the great and noble horizons,
and had known the splendid vistas of the enlightened mind,
yet found that child-like beauty which rarely comes
into the soul of man.

On such as these, the cloth of poverty can outgrace
the robes of kings.

Fresco of St Francis at Subiaco,
painted shortly after his death

Grace Notes

O now for the heavenly grace notes,
giving accent to all things;
could man but tune his earthly story,
the harps of God might break their strings.

The Listener

I looked up to the vault of heaven;
I hoped to hear the voice of God,
but he spoke to me
from a hawthorn tree,
from a cricket in a nearby sod.
There, on my selfish mind it dawned
no words he keeps for me,
but listening still
I heard him speak –
through a bird, the wind, and a bee.

Make Time for Moments

Make time for moments of stillness;
deny for a while the pressures of living,
their vain excess.
Stop! and reflect in quiet on who runs the universe,
who is in charge at the end of Earth's day.

Dear God *

Dear God,
what a glorious life it's 'bin',
with its leaven of good,
its salt of sin;
the grace to forgive –
to remember to forget,
and a clasp or a kiss
before the sun has set.

Song of Life

This splendid life to its run of years,
youth and age, tears and laughter;
friends of the morning, friends forever,
friends now passed to the great hereafter;
what conceptions play the heartstrings,
touch the resonant chords of time;
what exceptions lift the moments
deathless from the dust and grime.

Every man to the Christmas portal,
every child to clasp a hand;
glee in heaven and woman immortal,
God abroad throughout the land;
live to the cracking life we savour,
live! live, live from the dawn to the stars;
great the hearts who sing with fervour
the songs of life to the last, last bars.

Think

Speak gentle since the days are short,
and spite is but the devil's sport;
though tempers flare to fiery need,
apologies can to friendships lead.

St Giles', St Peter's

St Giles', St Peter's
and high St Mary's;
St Saviour's, St Sepulchre's,
by faith man varies;
in towers and turrets
through all the shires,
and God to his merits
beneath bell-ringing spires.

All Saints', All Angels',
St Stephen's the stoned;
St Paul's, St Martin's,
Westminster, the enthroned;
St Jude's, St Michael's,
St Margaret's the Maid;
where weddings seem more holy
since most make the grade.

Recipe for Happiness

A bottle of brown ale, a glass,
a pipe and pouch of St. Bruno,
a piece of cheddar
and a cottage loaf;
paper, pen,
and the early hours before sunrise,
and a man could be sitting
and noting his thoughts
on the steps of Heaven.

The biggest mess since time began:
earth's shabby species – man.

Clodus Stupiditas

Their hope,
some fame, some glit of glory;
their need, the tinsel show;
their lives, a dull and unreal story;
their gift, no worth to show.

Vain fools,
for them the artful praises,
the invest word of guileful mind;
for them, the trough, the steamy haze;
for others, the caviar, wealth, and wine.

Hunt

Where battered hoof has struck the sward,
mute emblem of their fine propulsion,
the seedy rich for their reward
seek foxgut, blood, and hell's emulsion.

Critica Cranium Expandi *

O petty pomp, and consequence,
so stuffed with your own excellence;
how lucky me to be so dense,
nor drugged by my own eloquence.

Conclusions

What is ambition
but for witherings and rust,
by dais or by catafalque
to change and to dust?

January Sales *

I watch the bargain hunters
from the tarmac jungles,
eyes tiger bright,
a purse full of fangs,
searing the frowning fronts
beneath the neon signs;
all shapes and shames.
With grace of cats
they try the hats,
crimp the fabrics,
risk a smile to cramming mirrors;
there's room for errors
with vanity's fodder;
and harassed males stand lost
like relics from shrivelled wombs.
No male assumes his preference
where dainty claws
and scrubbers' paws
flick and flay;
say what scandalous price –
despite the clearing bait.
The fate of spring
moves turbulent
with each heap,
and hands leap
with raving strength
the linen mounds;
vague conceptions
brightening in each claiming breast.
There's little of rest
in this mad month.

Thesis on Psyche *

Life in the material sense
is a fragmentation,
a diffuse conception subtracted
from the primal origins
analysed of brief dissection
in some particular pass of time
where the quintessence
of living and matter has portrayed
the business of the universe
to a vague but culminate whole.
Whether in the psyche
or through the lesser meanderings
of the near conscious,
the mind extracts
from the mystique of dreams
the first fulminations
of the unsought vision,
this, the necessary criteria
to the wake-world thinker,
a means of application
to be set against the establishment
of accepted logic,
the common ground where lie
the seed-germs
of a final and reasoned equation.
But even here
one is only at the fringe
of strange thought fusions,
and there are only the symbols
of common realities
for the assembling to the chance probe
where mass drudge media
extrudes its thought singularities
which may or may not capitalise
on the structures of myth
in the relationship with sense.

All who are concerned with the sublime
and who have rejected the easy fatalism
of the humanities
must turn to this dream world,
the sequestered refuge
amidst the admixture
of day-thought and hard conception
where the images in flux
may be either forced or chanced
by time and fortune to crystallise
into signal appreciation
through the analgesic mists
of a strata'd intelligence.
Popular social reason
is ever the court
which indemnifies
the common identity
that contemporary society
in any age accepts
as being morally
or even theoretically sound.
In this state,
how is the psyche concerned
with dream analysis
in a relationship
which dispenses with the mind death
to break with the hard conformities
and draft conclusions
of organised animalism
and the levelled orders
acceptable in the laws
of corporate agreements?

Either we condition all thinking
in a mass-whole
of common generality,
or we commit the heresy
of individualism where the mind
rejects the close judgements
of the urbane sciences;
and in personal defiance
of human limiting factors
proposes a revelation
in its peculiar symbolic parlance
which could isolate it
from the pluralities
of practised erudition
and established thought.
The concept of being,
in this mortality
allied as it is
with fleshed intransigence,
being yet so conscious
despite the hysterias and obscurities
of the driven masses
herded by the neo-gods
of known history,
this concept feels only the oblivion
and the nullity of thought-force
where, in the cosmos
of mind and matter,
man has only to his ego – the doubt.

Conditions acceptable
to the plane of trained reason
are all too often chary
of those derivatives
thrown up in such mind formulas
as one sees in Blake,
or for that matter
those shock waves of analysis
relegated to the perusal
of earnest posterity
by Carl Gustav Jung.
We are familiar with
the establishments of form,
cryptic assessment,
and the judgements
of material success.
We know next to nothing
of that twilight empyrean
where the mind searches
among the stars
of its vision,
or the arid lunarities
of its vague psyche conscious.

March

Now comes March, the breezy month,
brazen and zesty as a heedless youth;
let us go now, let us turn for the deep woods,
down through the mossy grove
and there to see the proof
of the year's first probings;
nature's helmets by bole and bank,
rank on rank of flowered form
to break and line and probe all growth
with the pennantry of spring –
to fling the first timid fledglings
down the everywhere winds:
the scut of fur, blithe speed
through thicket and thorn;
and from deep retreats this life-burst green.

And so comes March, the robust consort,
hale and strong with the blast of his entry,
to drive as on the cavalry of storm
this last of the withering months;
and soon to let maid April waiting in the wings
make move with her humming host.
Rude friend pass now,
pass quick with your whistling keys,
your jangle of weathers;
pass with your skelter and racket and din,
with leaf of last year's ghost;
but go easy dour keeper at the gate of spring –
there's a primrose crowd at your feet.

Whispering Green *

Listen into the silence;
look to the green-growth,
this quiet of establishment
where the thorn is to breaking;
where brindled woods bend to sap-rise –
to the clean keen winds bringing hints
and promise of April's showers.

The year is on the move,
and algae'd pools brim by the greensward;
lambs skit and survey from old heaped dung
the bright new world; ewes stare –
they know this rare and opulent realm
of growth and song; the throng of summer
soon to dance and hum with tunes of life.

Wait! Listen into the silence;
these lowly levels of tuft and turf,
a mole's mound, the hedgehog haunt;
and soon to awakening, a dormouse move;
note fret and dart of small communities,
while overhead in the strengthening sun
the sable crow communes to wheel and call.

Listen into the silence;
to way of trees – these gnarled and ancient orders
that stride into distance;
things noble and alive, and loud with meaning;
the clues to revelation, to new beginnings;
and here to purpose, new teachings
at the threshold of high wonder
and the force of creation.

Thrush's Nest *

Moss-wound this secret
in a threat of thorn,
five blue pearls, meek April's gems
hid in the faint light,
staple to simplicity of heirs to the morning,
who watch with the lute in their throats;
who have whistled all dawns
to the coming of a flower,
the infancy of love once passed beyond thorn.

This thrush's nest;
speckled watchman of the dawn,
what diadems do you encrust with the stars;
what magnificence have you witnessed
beyond treasuries of earth;
man's battalions could be as dusts of the desert,
while you, frail brother,
you could be there at the adoration;
you could be there with the lamb.

Song Thrush

To Spring

O sigh for the spring,
for the sky blue note
of the cuckoo's throat,
for the sheen'd wing,
for brooding rooks
on piles of sticks,
for little brown birds –
their mating tricks;
for striving mole
and half-cut ricks,
for the steaming calf
which the dun cow licks,
for the glow of warmth
on slate and bricks,
for the power
which makes men sing.

When

When mornings fill with cuckoo cries,
when larks pour lyrics from the skies
and in the fields the daisies dance,
or so it seems in that first glance,
when beauty charms the ear and eyes,
where men are still and earth is wise.

When life reveals its gladdest hour,
when men feel that latent power
which discards dull and turgid things
and frees their souls to nature's wings –
ambition's prides are left undone
for life and truth have now begun.

May

Glorious May;
a joy's stride
through a rare kingdom;
this way of lamb-cry, foal-skip,
all the say and song of spring;
a primrose treat,
daffy-blown dells;
pipe, tweet, half-hidden bells
blue as heaven's vault.

This blossy tide,
borne as on zephyrs
by green banks;
first scents of summer,
and again, again
that haunting note:
cuckoo! cuckoo!
and the year
to all things young.

May blossom in Barton Seagrave

Swallows

Like darting fish,
the swallows skim through groves of lucid air
made warm by late June suns.
Winging wraiths,
they cross the virgin forests of sedge,
of mallow, coltsfoot, and of bryony sweet;
all unspoilt still by beast or man.
Cleaving upwards, earth-shot bolts,
they spin in joys unbound;
wings that sport through the leaves of aspen,
that balm the evenings by my thatch,
and fill calm hours with sound.

Female Kestrel

The Falcon *

High in the braced heavens
the small dot turns on its wheel of flight;
skids through strata'd zones of light to a poise on rays;
sets that aquiline head to a gaze with the gods;
nerved unto violence again to that curve,
that swing through azured realms of grace to aired solitudes;
such movement, such balance; what smooth elegance there;
death's privateer hoist on random winds to his watch below.

Wind-poised to hold,
then the shut of pinions, remote and small;
the whip, the fall of death's live bolt;
phenomenal shaft and shock of speed;
a hostile hurtle down death's sheer drop, and smack!
So swift, so easy the white-ringed neck,
and smashed to smoke the blue-feathered grace from the elms,
the settling of the feathers by the copse.

November

I watch where fieldfares come in scurrying hosts,
all mute, they swoop the chill November sky,
silvered undersides, flit like banished ghosts
and soon are gone with never a parting cry.

The robin peeps and watches from the tree,
his head is still, his body rides the bough,
his eye is bright, and yet no word has he –
no greeting toot or chelp he gives me now.

Where the hedge is black, berries like scarlet suns
enliven scenes that knew of glories gone,
and where skies weep and swelling waters run
floods now rave, and then go plundering on.

Poplars stand like witches' brooms against the sky
all stark and shorn of summer's velvet green,
and moles now break the ground and wonder why
the world's so changed where they had lately been.

Fieldfare

Mountain

Speak from the mountain,
shout to the low hills –
no one hears;
only the eagles,
and God.

'Young Eagle in the Cairngorms'

The eagle's eyrie is a lonely place,
but from it much can be seen…

In Fen Country

Green corn, to shimmering heat
and far off, the settled farms
clear and defined to fen horizons;
and to this, the perpetuity of earth
and truth and season with bird and bee,
frond and flower to ultimate systems
where even man will stay his hand,
press his affairs that the spirit may steep.

What worth the days if lost that voice
whose utterance speaks from calm,
tells of established things like wings set free;
and only this heed still hard for the solace of pride;
and kingdoms forgotten where centuried fame
lays dust on cherished schemes;
a cavalcade to nothing,
a mirage of an unremembered dream.

Hearts long since – it seems they never die;
and while flowers have room their spirits will live,
the tomb and plot which holds that regenerate dust:
the common weed with the cloistered rose must flower;
and the breath of their living to an echo,
while words lend wings to the mind.

To no small fancy these meditate means,
yet substance and season make relevant
their truth to the heart.
And for just a while to stand in this deep green –
the mind quiet and conscious with words
amidst the vanities of living –
lost amidst the complex systems.

Green Clerestory *

My altar,
the still horizon shrouded as yet
by the slow dawn mist;
My east window,
daybreak and first light
lifting in the eastern sky;
My candle,
solitary star above the changing colours
and mishades of light;
My chancel,
the undersides of small clouds
like cherubs tinted by the unborn sun;
My choir,
the faint whisperings from the woodside
before the swelling chorus of the fields;
My bells,
the tink and tipple of clear water
to wimple by sand-shoal and pebbles;
My incense,
the breath of the rose blushed among thorn
on the cool dawn wind;
My benediction,
the dew on the bramble like agony
and the last lonely sweat of Christ;
My sacrament,
thc leaf of the lily and the blood-sap of the berry
crushed to my lip;
My submission,
a posy of cowslips and harebells,
with all the flowers of heath and field;
My recessional,
a retreat in solitude for renewal,
among nature's scenes and sound;

My blessing,
the knowledge and acceptance
of what has been and will be,
and of these to content myself.

Litany of the Still

To be alone and to be still;
to let the world for the while go by;
and there, no will for its frail success,
its need for transitory fame:
only sky – and natural things,
the cry of a seabird riding the wind;
a ply of waters to the purpose of tides,
and moments to culminate the need
where a spirit folds back the deed of time.
Only this, the prime of living when hands are still;
when the will subscribes to a healing force
whose latent powers endorse this search of man
for reason, for entirety and birth.

To be alone and to be still;
and far-off the first grey strata'd hints of day;
a mind condensed for clues
where powers and universe
beckon to fulfilment, to revelation and light;
this need of the spirit to sight again
those vistas prominent and profound;
and only the sound of the morning bird
to herald once more the litany of the still.

Wild Rose

Wayside flowers dew-flecked from night,
to solitude bring such inward sight;
as notes each frail and morning span
might frond with light the soul of man.

Let eyes look once on scenes of grace;
slight nature's head and lifted face;
a fragrant waft that drifts the thorn,
a wild rose blushed and virgin born.

Dog Rose

Pansy Flowers

Soft purple, elf satin,
streaked yellow and hue,
like cloaks of kings
or the fallen wings
of angels earth could not bear;
and where a comelier flower,
a daintier seat of beauty
pearled with dews,
low courtiers bowed in grace
to the lonely rose.

Simple Things

Each little flower that blooms
shall find its place appointed,
by one who tends and grooms
which he alone anointed.

Each little bird that wings
through heaven's blue striated,
its impulsed throat it sings
where God its voice imparted.

Each pebbly-bottomed stream
that through the years hath wandered,
to carry its living gleam
where sweetness ne'er was plundered.

Each green and mossy bank
where little creatures scampered,
to climb through grasses rank
and lead their lives unhampered.

All noble things in life
'twas God alone created,
and man that brought the strife
when God's good things he hated.

In Early Light

In early light,
before the level smoke of village fires
with spreading table leaves the mist,
or distant yard cock clangours his bugling charge
to the shutters of night,
I stand in universe, silent;
lonely to thought by the bargains of green,
and the world asleep away,
with the stream mist winding its swathe
over close, meadow, and drippings of woods.

Only in the time of silence
are we permitted the long visions,
the close communion with the beginning,
and the world with its hours –
clear in rebirth.

The strange formulas in the child-light
shaft to the prisms of perfection,
and man is at knowledge with the first factors;
eyes fused in the furnace of the dawn.

The Horse

And who made the flowers
and the children to sing,
the rose in the thorn
and the lark on the wing?

And who made the lion
and the whale in the sea,
the scents of high summer
where the winds blow free?

And what great mind
here stayed its course
to make such beauty
as we see in a horse?

And what being moved
beyond earth's claim
so fashioned earth's flesh
on a heavenly frame?

And what grand stroke
in a moment rare
set poetry to gallop
on the plains of the fair?

And then what hand
from a free-blowing mane
let man make a halter,
a bit, and a rein?

New Forest Pony

Where Plovers Fly *

Only the slow clop
of a horse's hooves walking a quiet road;
the grind of wheels
where iron gravels its way over stone;
only an old man,
the fragrance of smoke from his pipe;
a weathered face
like a bound book, worn and well used
in the library of life.

Only the move of winds,
the swee of chaffinch over thistles and thorn;
a ripple of corn
browned ripe for the nodding machines;
only the means of men
to earth and to trades
where destinies of nations lie;
where the ply of hands
are to future schemes;
or to a prayer in a field –
where plovers fly.

Jordan in England

Let us walk through the deep meadows,
along by the bullock-pad turf
to the gravel shallows where the images lie,
where the music of the midge broods calm,
where water lips in the language left by boys
who have long grown old,
who have hid their summer's dreams
under the mossed and secret pebbles.

Unstrange, the knowing then,
and still unstrange each image
that sprites the stream:
church, stone, and foreign field
contain their dust;
and bells of home fling echoes
that scatter down time.
But listen!
Hear the small riots
of the sprinkle-foot hours;
there is no death;
only man's time,
a little of waiting,
and baptism of boys
by the Jordans of England.

The Fly

December's fly,
wizened as a currant, utterly dead,
all members dry.
A sigh
where naked winds avaunt
the winged desperado's tossing to the south
a bird-flung sky.

And I,
of the blinding sap which spins my vein
again trade glance with death's dry husk,
only a fly,
and summered fields flooded with gold,
fold on fold of June's full pain
priced a vision – a vista'd scene.

Wings.
No more they tint to a year's high sun
what spring's begun this month shall see undone,
the black wood's fortunes slough in mouldering host
and the minute ghost,
drained of the spidering tongue.

Rubbish Tip

Bizarre world of rejected things;
society's surplus, coagulation of colour;
of bumblebees about their business,
of the blue-bummed preacher fly
squatting, still, on his poppy pod pulpit;
sad banks of sawdust,
flesh from the forest souring in the sun.

Wreaths of wire, rusting;
insolent rat ubique, sneering, peeping,
scampering across the heaps of tin, tarpaulin, tyre;
seeming to laugh at the milk-voiced maid,
the bob-haired Borgia who lays poison,
who smiles and dreams of love.

Plush plumes of thistle, pendants of hazel;
no need their seed the distant fields,
no need to wander, so much to hide.

Gloves in the Barn

Like bats,
the old leather gloves hang hard,
set in the dried strong sweat
of decayed time, rust-flaked tools,
museum poised,
with the deep-thumbed stamp
of the breath-starved bankrupt,
the rural patriarch
who made one deal with death –
who waits in a market of stones.

Rotten-beamed barns
mute as corpses,
and dry bones crumbled
in a flesh of stone;
bull-head nails, stiff like troops
in the toffee tins of a lost childhood
where the spider stirs the dust,
the brooding dark –
the grumbling years groan on.

Repose

The bird on the nest
the child at rest
and all is still.

A hope will keep
thro' nightlong sleep
with God until...

The morning star
we see from afar
as perched on hill.

With faith of a child
so meek, so mild
that heeds thy will.

My cares are thine
thy love is mine
all's calm and still.

Bed

This billowing nest
wherein men howl to life;
the bane of crowding
childhood's eager years;
the place wherein
men dream in secret worlds;
the apt compelling couch
for passion's force;
the night galleon
that meets tomorrow's tide;
the sheeted bench
where old men take their leave;
mute alpha and omega
of men's days.

Sleep

Let here the heed of day
and the trammelled mind
ease to night's black shades;
let now the last hard claims of day
reject the harrying scheme;
here to no vague intrusion
with misted scene infused by calm,
that they the tightened grasp might ease;
and day-hard sense reject.

Let life's hope and purpose
to this dulled hour
in chasm'd deeps here plunge;
unferried by thought, uncared,
improvident of waking time;
let late phantasmal dreams
submerge their ploy,
that now the nocturne drape of hours
fold from the glit of day;
let the way of the stars herald silence,
and the mind be still;
and never a dream to disturb,
never a move –
but the rise, and fall, of sleep.

The Trinity *

The owl, the mouse, the parish priest;
of sober trinity which, the least,
of all the creatures here ordained
the church but three has still retained.
The mouse, he scuts amidst the pews,
scratches, scrapes, devoid of news,
of Sunday folk with human fault
who unload sin by rail and vault;
who never a crumb subscribe his need
except where flowers may drop their seed.
God lease man's bounty to this house
as times are tight for a sacred mouse.

The owl impoverished in the tower,
hunched, observes man's temporal power,
notes the heathen's crowded way –
and just the few who come to pray;
glaring with his watchman eyes
twits and tuts when someone dies,
whose slow cortege with solemn tread
files inside behind the dead,
and then when all's for Heaven equipped –
he vomits bones in his high crypt,
shuffs and fluffs his lonely state,
sees the worldlings through the gate,
sees his henchmen belted, black,
fee'd and silent hastening back.
State temporal makes its mild excuse
and mist soon hides the small recluse.

'Wood Mouse saying his Prayers'

The priest in this his holy state
sees his flock in ardent spate;
logic now rejects confession,
quiet he to smart profession;
careful with his 'local bosses'
heeding hints of likely losses,
where by word or thought implied
the dwindled flock could soon divide,
and so in pulpit heights alone
he prays for souls and crumbled stone;
midst tangent faith and varied creed
more faith he needs – more faith indeed,
for what with death-watch in blest ribs,
quotas, quotes, and life's ad-libs,
satanic interest here it seems
submits its proof of Satan's schemes,
invests and fills the bingo halls,
crowds the pubs, exalts the pools,
gilds with light life's broader way,
spurning priest and systems grey
alone for him the decent garb –
slight armour, 'gainst earth's varied barb;
vast change decrees the rock must break
and plate glass please for Jesu's sake;
the heedless throng to milling slope
make shout and rant and downward grope,
for who need fear what all know well –
the priest is wrong and earth is hell.

The Abattoir *

Enter with awe the temples of stench,
these bowel-gas precincts of the late dumb friends;
could they have known death so quick from the frenzy,
the glazed fear and fret, from the struggle to the bolt?

Steam-halled, hose-washed, now to hang in fleshed glory;
draped majesty assured, head-halved and down-cleaved:
pearl-slack internals to shine with pale beauty –
flaccid, slab-scraped, the dumb virgins of doom.

By this, the hooked piece of flesh and blood-wash,
the white-capped deciders divide for man's need;
dissected by portions availed not to cautions
where knives flick and flay – in deft trade, and speed.

Sugar-pig and farm-friend, the pink myths of childhood;
how serious these matters to decide the full man:
choice meats for blending, red flesh for rending,
and bright lights – for exits where wives pick and plan.

The Bird *

Better the eye to close
like that of a bird
when the flying is done,
when it no more may rise
to meet the sun,
nor view the familiar scenes
of field and home.

Strange is life
when hearts matured and tempered
take their leave;
and for those who grieve
it matters not this pass of years;
tears are as showers –
brief in the sun they shine and fall,
yet as dew in the dawn
life waits its cue,
this onwardness of time.

The prime of our living
is but for decay,
a moment to incandescence
fused with light;
and before the night,
the expectations of a day
comes the simplicity of truth;
the close of an angel form
as with the death of a bird.

Pool

This is the pool
where the dragonfly skims,
where beauty brims
to the blue fly's murmur
and broods to bladed reed,
where weed and a water's whopple
point the pike
who sulky seeks the stippled shallows,
bursts death fierce in tiger charge –
scoops the fretting fry.

Time's waters cool:
life nerved and quick
in death's stale pool;
the genesis jungles
formed of sallow and sedge;
the spider spinning the harp of death
may dance and devil those mocking strings,
and the lyre that strums
when zephyrs sigh
will break with beauty's husks and wings;
so falls the dust
of a myriad wishes,
so scums the shore
when the pike's tail swishes.

The Bond

This constant bond within the heart,
whose force true friends may merit –
the glow which warms the inward part
and lights the human spirit.

The kindled gift from childhood's time,
the stay, through change and weather;
the bond which lasts through life and prime
which only death can sever.

This binding truth and force in man,
beyond realm or pride or glory;
the lamp which lights his mortal span
to take beyond death his story.

Some word which lives when lips are still,
some love death may not banish;
the eternal fire, the immortal will
supreme 'til earth shall vanish.

Trade not cheap this fountainhead,
this crystal spring of beauty;
'twere better the words were left unsaid
than slight the soul of duty.

What utterance proves in man the means,
he lisps alone his story;
yet he alone transcends the scenes
to strike his line of glory.

Breathe soon the word that turns the prayer,
so God with man in union
shall yet rejoice and with him share
Christ's one and true communion.

This constant flame within the heart,
whose force true friends may merit –
the glow which warms the inward part
and forever lights the spirit.

Friends

A glass of wine,
the warmth and welcome of friends;
a smile which discards the years,
clears the sward of life
like frost before the sun.

One moment where the minds
in retrospect see the whole, the truth of life;
and there to utterance as like a child
in the spontaneity of its waking prayer;
the rare impassioned moment
where mind and heart are annealed
in such delight as mocks the froward shades of loss,
or of death.

This grace, this blessed concept
of having known life's brief;
this love and link where hearts in truth
have qualified grief,
have forged the strength which delineates more
these gentler bonds;
and on where the tested thread
has knitted through life,
the fabric of friends.

Hunstanton *

Just we two, and the host
we have known: the loves
and the lovers of long ago;
those who had walked this way,
left their whispers in the wind
to blow like echoes from the heart
by this the timeless move
of the sea.

For what is worth or living
in this bliss of days;
all things, all ways are circumscribed
to the knowings of the heart,
yet these images fixed and still
in time are forever;
cherished and lovely
by this whispering sea.

Hunstanton Cliffs *

Just the two of us,
and the sounds of the sea;
a loose-pebbled shore
to green-cushioned rock;
footprints in sand
untouched by this day's tides;
a running sea for winds and weathers,
drift and cacophony,
where seabirds lift to haunt and cliff –
the crumbled faults of impermanence
to fracturings of time.

Buds

Come, my heart, to yet untrammelled glades;
let's walk awhile where the love we'd known was young;
where flowers bloomed in fields where no sun fades,
nor seared with heat the cups where bees would tongue.

Let there earth's joys recede like a faded night,
and common thoughts be lulled on the dying breeze;
then be my love with me to the coming light,
and simpler joys be leased to hearts at ease.

The Awakening

Gone is the light of earth's old morning,
the angel horns shall break with sound;
and the sleepers leap to that first warning
where the cry of the soul from death's unbound.

No more this earthward sun their vision
shall cross again his temporal rays,
for the final hosts now seek admission
to the glory of God with hymns of praise.

The heavens are rent, earth's constellations
shall fade and pass as in the night;
and the throated organ's full ovations
shall swell to the gates of eternal light.

Inklings of Heaven

How fair this land where the children dance,
these quiet lanes and charms and spires half-hid;
the fields and farms, the flowered dell of child and daises,
the songs of school; and nearer, the stream and willowed pool
where dallied the hours; where lived the scenes of childhood,
and gathered its flowers.

How fair the land with its villages and homes;
slow lanes for lovers, green haunts, yellowed stone;
the jewels and gems of England to adorn the fading light,
and the night to enshroud a sunset;
glint with fire the wind-cock in the deepening rays.

How fair my country, here to have walked;
to have known and to have paused amidst the changing scene;
so brief were the days, and life but a glance;
a chance where beauty revealed her buds and flowers
to this abiding grace;
a place for man and his child
to have known in a measure of days;
with ways to have followed,
to first inklings of Heaven.

Wollaton Wood *

Here was the heaven
which we boys knew then,
a something we have lost
now we are men;

the place we may cherish
but no way to return,
for dreams only perish
in this loss that we learn.

Edale *

To the distances of earth –
of hill and sky;
and the mind to calm,
made clear while nature
reveals her loveliness.

And just awhile
to exclude from the throng
this microcosm of solitude,
with earth to its waking wonder –
like I saw it when a child.

Looking towards the Vale of Edale
from Mam Tor

Tea Cosy *

I see my mother's teapot still,
and the kettle simmering by the hearth;
for now it is in later years
such simple things have great worth.

We brothers then were young indeed,
our mother sweet, our father strong;
but now I often feel the need
of some dear word that left their tongue.

Old memory brings me still that joy,
which oft a boy at school I knew,
who loitered home to the scent of toast
and the cosy teapot's amber brew.

Now, I see the children with their cups,
they read the leaves as we did then;
Ah! Could they know the splendid pain
that memory brings now we are men?

The Willow Stream *

When we were boys, and lived those hours
for which men strive throughout their days,
I gave no thought nor sought a coming morn,
but what that haze unveiled more dreams
endowed from careless thoughts;
now I know the wealth I have left
in those far courts.

From the green-hid shallows
came the piping flute,
the lazing turn of the fin;
and the willows bowed in reverent grace
to the spring's unmuted din;
it was nature's joys unfettered there
by the fumbling themes of men;
and the happiest hours of all my days,
I realise now, were then.

Now I would walk *

Now I would walk in the fields of my God
and here no bee may bruise a flower
nor sully with ardent tongue that nectared trove;
no child's eye shall reflect the image of angels,
for these they are, and their raiment shall be
like gossamer in a summer's morn,
more fragrant than a night-borne rose.
Flowers they shall not pluck, for earth no more
may bleed from the innocent thought,
and dreams shall be time's vernal springs
soon gathered into seay calms.
The clouds will lilt with laughter
and the woods beckon to their singing shades.
How sweet my earth where yet no blade
shall swathe the whispering choirs,
no furry ear quest long the sighing hours
nor dispute death
on the cool and morning wind.

Death

Welcome friend,
and now of this the load I bear
I pray accept;
not there with thee these late-year griefs,
nor the stare where alien faces
drift like ghosts;
the host I knew has long since passed,
and memories cast but shadows now
in this my winter of life.

Friend, no more the strife
where those strong hands my way shall guide,
but let the tide from that far shore
take this my dross; and no loss mine
when there before the light may shine
where hope holds high its brand of flame
and the far horizon glows with living fire.

Midnight

In this scheme of things
where understanding fails,
the end of all conclusions of heart and mind;
there, this spirit poised for regions
where no companion hand clasps its comfort
when I go.

The Lord be my stay,
my hope at last,
the only hold I have on this life's course,
and take this remnant worn and frayed with years,
the husk I bring, alone,
in fear and fault.

Be thou there
that instant when I break,
hold fast the failed fragment that I am;
and from these faded glories sensed in earth,
let me with those I loved
see but thy face.

Child Burial *

And was this the test,
the cross and the faith,
God's promised fulfilment –
the sweat, and the wraith;
the smashed tossed hell
through the wrack and the tears;
the bloody assize
at the gate of the years?

The little pink rose
peeps from the thorn
and the forest of death
crowds in the dawn;
the dominions of mercy
no language can find
to scourge the chill rot
that the womb has defined.

O teachings of Jesus,
the hope glowing strong
amounted to this –
a mound two feet long.
Come tears and damnation,
this cross life endowers;
and love's mothering earth –
soon smothered with flowers.

Two Summers Gone *

Child, from pain's low hill go now;
go with your crown and tribulation,
an infancy flower in earth's slight tenancy
to preclude all sin;
life's season was not for you,
nor the wreath of age
to cumber that angel brow;
like the plucked spring flower you are
for the cherub host,
and life's late tears are to nothing
where rays of brightness fall,
light the sunbeam roads of children
onto the fields of praise.

Child, from earth's small death
take life, unblemished to live;
enter that gentler realm
where all the children play,
where neither grief nor hurt
again shall bruise your bud,
but leaves the tender flowering
for hearts that wait;
for hearts that shall warm
to those infant eyes,
when grief is done.

Snowdrops

These the little ones
who went so early,
they needed no lessons
nor vain promptings of life.

Not for them
the gathering of flowers,
the heed and hurt
of pride and powers.

A moment their wonder,
an awakening their mortality;
but they were for flowers
more fair than earth.

What tears were theirs,
they were as dew on spring's first buds;
just a dampening on petal'd forms
for their brief passing.

Life is a moment in a summer of dreams;
and for them there is no autumn,
nor late cry at the withering of the year –
only a meek conclusion, before the silence of the frost.

Snowdrops

Here is the way
where woodside waters
whisper in the language
of baptismal flood;
where the maidenhead blooms
of earth's early daughters
sprang the flowers of sorrow
from earth-common mud.

Here is a glory at hand
for the seeing,
a way of the heavens
to earth made known;
a time for man
and the child of his being
to see the first drifts
of wintering stone.

Sleep, my child

Sleep, my child –
sleep sweet where mother's laid thee,
and in thy dreams
go now to him who made thee;
so when the morning stars shall pale
and the sun must rise,
we'll know that night hath left no veil
before those eyes.

Look, my sweet –
look up to these who love thee,
and who would greet with eyes
like stars above thee;
who saw thy morning cloudlets bloom
in each sun-spun curl,
and knew that Christ left in this room
a priceless pearl.

The Warden

Bear me down lowly
sweet and sublime,
bear me down holy,
Lord in my prime,
calm as thy features,
words quietly said –
kind to your creatures
and peace in my head.

Bear me down lightly
with good my employ,
my faith glowing brightly
as when once a boy,
a stream for my Jordan
where cleansed my few fears
and Christ my true warden –
my love of past years.

Notes by nephew Graham

Helpston

Written at the graveside of John Clare in Helpston, near Peterborough, probably one Easter (additional title: *Easter Interlude*). Uncle Joe confessed to me that 'honey'd' wasn't quite the right word, because Northamptonshire limestone is grey, but he couldn't think of a better one. The cottage in which Clare spent the first forty years of his life is now preserved as John Clare Cottage, and is open to the public. *'So oft I leave'* (p. 3) could also be titled *Helpston*.

John Clare (1793-1864)

Dubbed Northamptonshire's 'peasant poet', John Clare undoubtedly appealed to Uncle Joe because he was a local, a labourer, and a genius with language, through which he expressed his love for the land and especially its birds.

Glinton

It was in the church at Glinton, next door to Helpston, that the boy John Clare was taught the three Rs. Uncle Joe added after the title: To the memory of John Clare.

Brigstock

An attractive limestone village surrounded by remnants of Rockingham Forest. The 'meadow stream' is Harper's Brook, which runs past a communal field known as 'The Meadow' and on through the village.

Bells o' Brigstock (original version)

Arthur Mee's guide to the counties of England, *The King's England*, states: 'The musical bells of its ancient tower are known far and wide in this fair countryside' (*Northamptonshire*, Hodder and Stoughton, 1961, p. 46). It's a ring of eight, with the tenor weighing 13 cwt.

A Verse Cameo on Brigstock

St Andrew's Church has notable Saxon features, such as 'long-and-short' stonework. On Hall Hill, the village centre, stands an Elizabethan market cross, where the May Queen from the primary school is garlanded each year and the children dance round the maypole (*The May Dance* (p. 12) and *The Queen of the May* (p. 13)). Bocase Stone (17th C.), on the edge of Fermyn Woods, marks the site of a tree where, it's thought, Norman courts were held. According to folklore, King John and Robin Hood were visitors – but not together!

The May Dance

The stackyard was where the farmer stored his hay. The ribbons refer to the children's maypole dancing on May Day, as recorded by the old photo (1932).

The Silver Band

Uncle Joe was a principal cornet player in Brigstock Silver Band, which practised in a cramped wooden hut ('hutch of sound'). The band would come out to play on a Sunday evening on Hall Hill, as portrayed in his picture 'Band Concert, Brigstock' (p. 15). Uncle Joe is directly in front of the man sitting on a chair. The word 'plaint' in the second main verse is poetical for 'lament', perhaps indicating the cornet's moving tone.

Christmas

Every year Brigstock Silver Band played carols all round the village on Christmas morning, striking up with 'Christians awake, salute the happy morn'.

Braybrook's Row and **Derelict Cottages**

Joseph's wife Marjorie was born at No.1, Braybrook's Row, a terrace of limestone cottages, adjacent to Spencer's Timber Yard, in Brigstock. Verse five of *Derelict Cottages* refers to the blitz on Coventry on 14-15 November, 1940, which could be seen and heard from Brigstock some forty miles away. Braybrook's Row was eventually demolished, so considering Uncle Joe's sentimental attachment to No.1, these must be his most nostalgic poems.

The Boxing Day Hunt

A long tradition in Brigstock is the Boxing Day Meet of the Woodland Pytchley Hunt on Hall Hill which, despite the current ban on fox-hunting, attracts a large crowd, including many from outside the village. We can only guess what he meant by 'round tally'. Could it refer to mustering or 'rounding up' the hounds by the hunting horn? Tally-ho, we know, is the rallying cry of the huntsman when a fox is sighted.

The Old Dry Lane

'Oldry Lane' heads north out of Brigstock towards Fermyn Woods. Today it's literally bisected by a busy bypass, which robs it of some of its charm, but at least there's peace and quiet at the heart of the village these days.

The High Way

Problem: 'shed' and 'mead' don't rhyme (v. 3). Suggestion: since 'mead' is poetical for 'meadow', it would rhyme with 'shed' if it was pronounced as a shortened form.

Straight Riding

A straight mile-long track through the woods just north of Brigstock.

On Silver Hill

Silver Hill is a gently rising grassy field on the outskirts of Brigstock.

Sawmill

Spencer's Timber Yard harvested trees from Rockingham Forest. Brigstock's skyline was dominated by a giant crane which moved tree trunks into the sawmill. The crane was dismantled when the timber yard relocated.

The Small Friends

Marjorie and Joe had a succession of dogs and cats. Ranee, Badger and Judy were their dogs, and Tony, Charlie and Ben were mine – of whom they were equally fond. In his painting 'The Friends', Uncle Joe imagines several of the pets playing on his front lawn.

Golden Labrador

Judy was their last, much loved dog. This touching little poem is a modest conflation of two very similar versions.

The Organ Blower

For many years Aunt Marjorie was organist at St Andrew's Church, Brigstock. For much of that time the organ was blown manually by depressing a lever to inflate the bellows – the louder the music the greater the effort required. Uncle Joe took his turn on the rota. The words 'enscent' and 'enmove' I take to be poetic licence. Then 'enmove' may mean that his spirit was lifted, inspired by 'the evening hymn', or that he felt removed from the cares of the world.

Weathercock

Image: the weathercock on St Andrew's Church, Brigstock. Perched at 90 feet or thereabouts he enjoys a commanding view over the village.

Down a Country Road

Also titled *Winter*. A shorter version, titled *Brigstock*, identifies where he had in mind.

Before the Sun

Also titled *Nocturne and Mirage*. Cf. Psalm 19.1: 'The heavens declare the glory of God; And the firmament shows His handiwork' (NKJV). Unfortunately, since the poem was written, the night sky has become fainter in built-up areas due to increased light pollution.

Quarries

Uncle Joe worked for a time on the railway at Corby Steelworks, where local ironstone was smelted by blast furnaces ('iron-skirt maidens') into so-called pig iron and then oxidised into steel. 'The long-lost wood where the toothed bucket grabs for a forest's feet' could refer to the roots of the original Rockingham Forest cleared for agricultural use before mining for iron ore ('rough red rock'). 'Serration of furrow, scattered slabbed rock; feather of larch, of withering pine' almost certainly refers to the ridges and furrows thrown up as the overburden or spoil on top of the iron ore was deposited during the mining operation. 'Pickled dead sleeper, cast iron chair': the wooden railway sleepers were soaked in creosote to preserve them, and cast iron chairs were the U-shaped sockets that held the rails in place. 'Relics of old companies, lost in the amalgamations of year '22': since the context here is the railway, it must refer to the amalgamation of railway companies into 'The Big Four' by the Railways Act of 1921 (Hansard 1922), which took effect early in 1923. The 'bright vein of metal on flat ferrous floor' is presumably the iron ore at the bottom of the quarry. The 'signal plume' is the combined steam and smoke coming from the saddle tank locomotives, which burned top quality coal from Wales ('bright Welsh wealth'). The 'high tubs' are the large wagons which carried the iron ore to the furnaces. 'The minotaur tread': an apt simile for the dragline, a hefty excavator whose bucket was operated by a wire cable, described in verse one. The plant closed in 1980.

Welland Valley

Uncle Joe was especially fond of this lovely area between Northamptonshire and Rutland (see what he said about it in the Introduction). 'Brown stone': the belt of limestone which runs through Northamptonshire contains a band of ironstone in the Corby area, which provided attractive building material as well as ore for steel-making. 'The viaduct chain' is the Harringworth Viaduct: completed in 1878, three-quarters of a mile (1.21 km) long, with 82 arches striding the Welland Valley, it's the UK's longest masonry railway viaduct.

Wansford Bridge

On one copy of this poem Uncle Joe typed the title *The Forgotten Railway Line*, and then added in writing, 'Wansford to Stamford'. The 'small bridge' must therefore be the one down the A47 over the old Wansford to Stamford railway line, which closed in 1929. One detail that doesn't fit, though, is the notice banning traction engines, which was only on the impressive twelve-arch bridge over the River Nene in Wansford itself. 'No coupling clank nor squeal of flange': as the train pulled away, the slack in the couplings between the wagons or coaches made a clanking sound; round a tight bend the wheel flanges 'squealed' as they scraped against the rails.

Fotheringhay

Fotheringhay is a small, attractive village with an imposing collegiate church by the River Nene. It became famous for its castle with royal connections, including the birthplace of Richard III and the gift of Henry VIII to Catherine of Aragon, who is buried in nearby Peterborough Cathedral. But it gained notoriety for the execution of Mary Queen of Scots in 1587 on a charge of treason. All that remains is a grassy mound where thistles grow, and a block of masonry. Mary was buried in Peterborough Cathedral, and later in Westminster Abbey.

That Loving Chapter

Written in honour of King George VI at the time of his death (6th February, 1952).

At the Passing of a Beloved Monarch

The King was an emblematic leader of his people during the Second World War ('through years more terrible than any known').

Airfield (Grafton Underwood)
and **Grafton Underwood (Airfield)**

These two poems commemorate the American Servicemen who were stationed at Grafton Underwood in Northamptonshire during the Second World War, from where they flew B-17 'Flying Fortresses' on bombing raids over German industrial and military installations. One of them, Brooke Diamond, from Florida, married Marjorie's sister Nancy.

Rothwell Crypt

An unusual feature of Holy Trinity Church, Rothwell, is its 13th C. charnel house, one of only two in the country – a vault containing hundreds of human bones and skulls, probably transferred from disturbed graves, and possibly where pilgrims prayed for the dead among the dead in medieval times.

The Witness

Also titled *The Midwife*. Uncle Joe wrote to me, saying: 'I've got something together about the woman from the inn who tended Christ and Mary at the time of his birth. She seems to have got left out of things a bit.' (According to legend it was St Bride.) There appears to be three quite different versions of this poem, one of which is longer.

Easter Day 1969

Siloah, or Siloam, was one of the main sources of water in Jerusalem. Its supply could be intermittent. The Pool of Siloam came to be used by the sick and others to wash in (John 9.7).

Follow Me

See Matthew 4.18-20.

Sally Army

The red shield is being phased in to replace the crest and was originally the symbol of the services provided, similar to the NAAFI, to members of the military and emergency Services in times of conflict.

For Kathleen Ferrier (1912-53)

Celebrated English contralto whose distinctive voice Uncle Joe loved.

Dylan Thomas (1914-53)

Swansea-born poet whose style Uncle Joe greatly admired. He even read his poetry with a similar lilt to Dylan Thomas's.

Francis Thompson (1859-1907)

English Poet – a 'down-and-out' for years, whose classic poem *The Hound of Heaven* describes the divine pursuit of the human soul.

Thoughts on St Francis of Assisi (1181/2 -1226)

Tribute in prose to a popular saint who exchanged wealth for the service of the poor, and regarded all creatures as his brothers and sisters.

Dear God

'bin': slang for 'been'.

Critica Cranium Expandi

A waggish riposte when a bit of a clever Dick tried to put Joseph down as a bit of an ignoramus.

January Sales

In Uncle Joe's time it was a once-a-year sell-off after Christmas – the cause of 'stampedes'! The present day equivalent is 'Black Friday'.

Thesis on Psyche

Your guess is as good as mine!

Whispering Green

Also titled *March*. There's a slight problem over the word 'sable' in verse three. Another version adds 'in flight', so we know it's talking about a bird. A further version has 'the sheened and sable communes . . .', indicating that 'sable' is an adjective. Adjective followed by verb implies a missing noun – 'crow' maybe. Then it would read: the sable crow communes to wheel and call. Other suggestions welcome.

Thrush's Nest

In Clare's poem of the same name, the nest lining of 'wood and clay' is rotten wood pulp and mud. He also correctly identifies the female as the nest builder.

The Falcon

This is a good example of how Uncle Joe might revise one of his poems. Sifting through the huge amount of material he left I found four versions of the second verse. Each one follows a similar outline, but the phraseology varies considerably. I've chosen the one I like best.

Green Clerestory

Also titled *In Green Aisles*. Clerestory – a series of windows in the upper section of the nave of a church.

Where Plovers Fly

Cover picture: 'Forget Me Not' – female Lapwing (Green Plover) with Field Forget-me-not. The breeding population has suffered such a significant decline in recent years that it's now on the Red

List – a cause for serious concern.
The 'swee of chaffinch' is the call of the male bird.

The Trinity

Nearly omitted for its scathing satire, but included for its brilliant wit. Is there irony even in the title too? He certainly touches on traits which are unworthy of the Church. Possibly a little poetic licence here too: Barn Owls, as the name suggests, will roost and nest in buildings, including church towers, while it's the Tawny Owl that 'twits' ('tu-whit'). Wood Mice will also enter buildings.

The Abattoir

Uncle Joe's poems are mostly idylls, but we've included a few polemics, such as this one – brilliant writing, despite a gruesome subject. Years ago there was a slaughterhouse near the middle of Brigstock, where you could hear the pigs squealing as they were being killed.

The Bird

A rather poignant comparison between the evanescent life of a bird and the transience of our own human nature (cf. Matthew 10.29).

Hunstanton and **Hunstanton Cliffs**

Hunstanton was Uncle Joe's nearest seaside resort. It's noted for its unique stripy cliffs of rusty brown, brick red, and off-white.

Wollaton Wood

Uncle Joe mentions in the Introduction that Wollaton Park in Nottingham was a place of inspiration in his formative years.

Edale

An area of outstanding natural beauty in the Peak District.

Tea Cosy and **The Willow Stream**

Two appealing examples of Uncle Joe's nostalgia. There are four slightly different versions of *The Willow Stream*, and it's difficult to know which he intended as the final one. For example, a typed version of line 5 is: 'endowed from waking thoughts'. So I've taken the liberty of modestly conflating them into something I hope Uncle Joe would approve of. Certainly to me verse two of *The Willow Stream* is his poetry at its most fluent.

Now I would walk in the fields of my God

'seay': 'sea' used as an adjective.

Child Burial and **Two Summers Gone**

Marjorie and Joe had one child, a daughter stillborn. *Child Burial* and *Two Summers Gone* are surely Uncle Joe's most moving poems, and so beautifully written. The same sentiments are encrypted in *Snowdrops* (pp.122,123).

My thanks to local historian Carl Hector for information on Brigstock; to Brian White, Hon. Museum Curator of the Nene Valley Railway, for clarifying *Wansford Bridge*; and to Dr Stephen Bell (nephew) and Billy Dalziel, Corby Borough Council's Heritage Development Officer, for explaining aspects of *Quarries*.

Page **Title** and first line